The Song of Songs is one of the great

has been a source of great blessing an

with the Lord Jesus. To meditate on this inspired text is to witness the unveiling of the beauty of our heavenly Bridegroom and to be drawn into greater intimacy with Him.

Nancy Leigh DeMoss
Author, *Revive Our Hearts* radio host

Iva has done a wonderful job of exploring the depths of the Song of Solomon in a way that certainly will encourage women. Iva is a wonderful communicator of the Word of God. She teaches and writes in a way that will pull you into the written Word as well as confront you with the question of your obedience to the precepts and principles found on its pages.

Amy Barron, Director of Women's Ministries
Kirby Woods Baptist Church, Memphis, TN

Shepherd-Shaped is a must-read for every woman who is weary of the wounds caused by the feelings of inadequacy, restlessness, competition, and conformity which characterize our culture. In it Iva May refreshes our memory of the Song of Solomon and the acceptance our Beloved has for the Shulamite. In doing so she applies to these hurts the healing salve of God's Word. As a pastor my desire is that each woman in my congregation read this book and allow our High King of Glory to display His affectionate love to her.

Jim Collier, Pastor
Oakhurst Baptist Church, Clarksdale, MS

The desire to gain acceptance is a common yearning in the hearts of all women. Women live in a world in which love is offered with conditions; the opportunity to experience unconditional love truly is rare. Iva's book offers fresh insight on the acceptance and love of God through this unique perspective on the Shulamite story. As you read, hopefully "the veil' will be pulled back so the joy and contentment of fellowship with God will begin.

Lisa Reavis, Pastor's Wife and Director of Ladies' Ministries
North Jacksonville Baptist Church, Jacksonville, FL

Printed in the United States of America
by Versa Press
Cover design by Dennis Davidson

All Scripture quotations, unless otherwise indicated on page
11, from the NEW AMERICAN STANDARD BIBLE.
Copyright 1960, 1962, 1963, 1968, 1971, 1972, 1973, 1975,
1977, by the Lockman Foundation. Used by permission.
Library of Congress Control Number 2006937272
ISBN 0-929292-79-0

Hannibal Books
P.O. Box 461592
Garland, Texas 75046
1-800-747-0738
www.hannibalbooks.com

TO ORDER ADDITIONAL COPIES, SEE PAGE 256

Shepherd-Shaped:
I Am My Beloved's, and He is Mine

*A Woman's Look at
the Song of Songs*

IVA G. MAY

Dedicated
to

the Shulamite woman who walked before me
—my mom and poet, Joyce Guy.

the Shulamite woman who walked beside me
—my friend, Lynn Lindsey.

the Shulamite woman following behind me
—my daughter, Jennifer May.

and to my earthly beloved,
—my husband, Stan May.

Acknowledgements

When our house burned in 2003 and I saw the scorched and shriveled remains of my computer, I thought I had lost all of my research for this book. Dennis Lee, thank you for doing the impossible—for rescuing my research from the hard drive of that computer!

I owe my gratitude to the women at Immanuel Baptist Church in Olive Branch, MS, for embracing my first attempt at teaching this material. Thank you for your encouragement.

I confess to my family, I am a computer hog! Thank you for the many hours you sacrificed Internet service and your own, personal use because I was on the computer!

My husband's secretary, Camille Couch, spent many late nights correcting my punctuation and grammar. Thank you.

The enthusiasm from my discipleship girls, especially Donna Enoch, Stephanie Schafer, and Jennifer Washburn, encouraged me that women need and want the message of this book.

To my four "Amen" sisters—Donna Gaines, Susan Cherry, Suzanne Grigsby, and Lynn Lindsey—thank you for your affirmation.

Thanks to my father-in-law, Skeet May, for believing in this book and helping make it a reality.

I could not have written this book without the encouragement of my husband, Stan. Thank you for allowing me to be a Shulamite woman.

Contents

Introduction

Every woman is shaped by something: hopes and dreams, the past, trauma, family, gossip, education, decisions (both good and bad), geography, ethnicity, and so forth. Even stories shape our lives.

Years ago when my daughter, Jennifer, and my oldest son, Jonathan, were 4 and 2 years old respectively, my in-laws for Christmas gave them a VCR and *Cinderella* video. We lived in rural Arkansas, where we received only one TV channel and that with poor reception. I lost count of the number of times they watched *Cinderella*. I did not know the impact of this video until late spring, when a salesperson knocked on our screen door and asked the children (who were playing in a clothes basket near the door) if their mother was home. Without batting an eye, my daughter, who that morning already had been disciplined several times, answered, "No, but my mean, ugly stepmother is."

Remember the story of Cinderella? She is trampled by her ambitious stepmother and stepsisters. Overworked while her stepfamily enjoys an extravagant social life, poor Cinderella feels doomed to a life of service. With the aid of a good fairy and entrepreneurial mice, Cinderella overcomes difficult cir-cumstances and actually marries the prince—and they live happily ever after.

Everyone loves a good love story with a happy ending, especially if it involves an unlikely candidate for love and a prince or knight in shining armor who rescues and carries her away on a white horse. Bookshelves in bookstores and libraries prove this obsession with love stories. Even in

Christian bookstores and church libraries Christian romance sections are heavily trafficked. If the modern Christian woman spent as much time in the Word as she spends in reading romance novels (both secular and Christian), she would be a wiser mother, wife, and friend. Not that reading romantic material is wrong, but dangers do lurk in escapes into fantasy. The imagination runs wild. Soon our realities (our marriages) become dull; discontentment sets in. Before long our spouses become less than they are because their flaws continually are compared to the handsome, perfect, romantic lead in the books we read.

Years ago I heard the late author and preacher Ron Dunn make an unforgettable statement of warning that forever impacted my life. If God granted us our fantasies, would they make or break us spiritually? Think about your longings— your fantasies. If God granted them, would they ruin your marriage, destroy your ministry, or put your walk with God on hold?

Ron's stinging words convict every daydreaming heart. While fantasies leave us empty, a love story told by God Himself captivates both heart and mind and brings joy and fulfillment. Solomon's Song is such a love story.

Because Solomon's Song of Songs is difficult to understand, the modern Christian woman often overlooks it. Traditionally this Song brings love and tenderness to the Jewish marriage. To protect the romantic and seemingly erotic phrases from misuse, the religious Jewish young man is not allowed to read this book until he reaches his 30th birthday. During the time of the Old Testament, women from nations surrounding Israel were seen as chattel—slaves or objects of man's pleasure to be discarded after use; by contrast married life in Israel represented the highest and deepest affection. To ignore this book is to miss learning and applying marvelous truths found in God's Word, both to the Christian marriage and to one's intimate walk with the Lord.

The Song of Songs, the most beautiful song, is the best of 1,005 songs (1 Kings 4:32) King Solomon wrote. Seven times in the song Solomon's name appears; five times the Beloved is referred to as *king* (1:4, 12; 3:9, 11; 7:5). It is the fifth of the poetical books following Job, Psalms, Proverbs, and Ecclesiastes. Portions of the Song are sung during the Feast of Passover. The main characters are Solomon, the Shulamite woman, and the daughters of Jerusalem, with various minor characters.

Historically the book is interpreted four ways:

- The glorification of wedded love (its literal interpretation);
- The relationship between Israel and Jehovah (its dispensational interpretation);
- The redemptive relationship between Christ and the Church (its redemptive interpretation);
- The communion between the individual and the Beloved, the Lord Jesus Christ (its moral or spiritual interpretation).

After reading dozens of books and commentaries, I am amazed to discover that of all the books written on the Songs, seldom is one written by a woman for women. As I repeatedly read the Song and thought about the stages of love and made application between the believer and Jesus Christ, I found myself personalizing it. The Song of Songs springs alive. From a practical standpoint this is the most intimate application a Christian can make of the book's teaching for his or her own life.

I can see myself in the Shulamite or can see a bit of the Shulamite in me: her struggle with inadequacy, her desire to belong to the most valuable person in the country—the king, her need for assurance, her struggle with intimacy, her questions and feelings of abandonment, her vulnerability and transparency with her companions. I see in her relationship with the Beloved many similarities in my own pilgrimage with the Lord. The relationship between the Shulamite woman and her Beloved clearly, helpfully, and thoroughly parallels the believer's walk with God.

In the same manner that her love relationship with her Beloved shapes and defines the Shulamite woman, so does our relationship with the Lord Jesus shape us—that is, if we allow Him and not other things to do the shaping. As I've already said, a multitude of things—his or her past, family, health, various crises, and so forth—shape each person. Paul exhorts believers to be conformed or shaped not by the world but by renewing the mind—that is, to allow the truth of God's Word to shape them instead. This story does just that.

The Song addresses the four fundamental questions that shape every woman's worldview:

- Who am I? What does being a woman mean?
- Where am I? In what kind of world do I live?
- What has gone wrong? Why do I experience pain and suffering?
- What can be done about it? What can I do to deal with (not eliminate) suffering and pain?

The *Song of Solomon* consists of a series of love lyrics. It is the lover, with heart enraptured, setting to music the thrill of the soul. Thus you have this cluster of song-flowers—each one setting forth some different phase of communion between the Beloved and the one so loved. The Shulamite woman in the Song of Solomon is a biblical Cinderella. Instead of a wicked stepmother and stepsisters, she has a mother and two half-brothers. She escapes the pains of reality (arduous work in the vineyard and pastures) by daydreaming about a relationship with the king.

Through this love story, filled with oriental imagery, numerous metaphors, and difficult-to-follow love songs, one may draw distinct parallels to the phases through which many believers pass in the Christian life. Through the life of the Shulamite we discover that she really is no different than today's modern woman. You, too, will discover a bit of the Shulamite within and experience similarities in the Heavenly Beloved's intimate relationship with you.

The Beloved takes the Shulamite where and how he finds her. He woos her and then marries her. The Song of Songs captures her various emotional experiences throughout their relationship: desire, delight, distance, discouragement, duty, and adversity. Her story plays out under the watchful eyes of her family, her companions, and the Beloved's friends. Application to nearly every phase every believer experiences, especially women on their spiritual journey and in their love relationship with the Lord Jesus Christ, are realized in this Song.

For clarity I have followed the New King James Version's assigned speaker parts for the entire Song. To honor copyright laws I have used the NKJV in chapters one, three, five, and six; the NIV in chapter two; the KJV in chapter four; and the NAS in chapters seven and eight. Let's get started.

The Shulamite

One day, while she rests beneath the shade of a tree, a young Shulamite woman dreams of her country's young and irresistibly handsome king. Dreaming offers hours of pleasant diversion from the drudgery of sheep-tending and vine-dressing and provides a harmless alternative to the harsh reality of her life. She fantasizes about what being romanticized by the king might be like. She envisions passionate kisses and words of delight. Even whispering his name gives her the shivers.

However, in the midst of the Shulamite's fantasies, reality breaks through like rain does on a picnic. It fills her mind with doubts about her appearance, her family, and her status in the community. A glimpse of her reflection in a nearby pool confirms her thoughts, as it reveals a sun-darkened complexion and rather average facial features. Manual labor also has been unkind to her hands and feet; all are calloused and stained with dirt. Sighing, she realizes that her dreams are just that—pleasant but hopeless notions. Her looks and station in life disqualify her as a recipient of the King's favor. She has nothing to offer and therefore will never capture the heart of the king. His eyes will never gaze in her direction. His search for a queen will be restricted to pale, manicured, and pedicured city girls. She sighs deeply with regret: her hopes and longings will always remain unfulfilled.

Each day disappears into the next until, suddenly, the unthinkable happens! Like a stone skipping across the surface of a pond, an approaching flock of sheep disturbs the Shulamite's contemplation. Looking up, she sees, of all people, the king and his herdsmen nearing the watering hole.

Panicked she hurriedly covers her head and rises to escape, but not before the king notices her face.

The king calls out, "Stay, don't run off." The Shulamite cannot help but obey his command and so lingers to talk. The two introduce themselves; the conversation turns to the weather and the sheep. Suddenly the time arrives for him to go. Each day afterward the king with his shepherds and flock appear at the same time, as she does with hers. At each encounter their conversation becomes more personal. One day she expresses her doubts and misgivings about her appearance. He quickly silences her negative description by describing what he sees, which is radically different from the pool's imperfect reflection.

Days pass into weeks as the Shulamite enjoys these daily visits. Imagine her astonishment when her family members reveal that the king has approached them and that arrangements have been made for a marriage! Thrilled beyond expectation, she agrees. After much celebration the two are married. As in every fairy tale, they live happily ever after—except that is not the end of the story. You see, only children believe in fairy tales. Listen closely as the story continues . . ..

The young bride loves living in the king's palace. Banquets are frequent. She entertains important guests and enjoys the clever conversation of high society. She bathes daily in fragrant oils and takes time to receive manicures and pedicures. Her skin becomes soft, smooth, and pale. She exchanges rough linen and wool for silk embroidered with gold and silver—designer-wear suited to a queen. Jewels adorn her wrist, neck, ankles, fingers, and nose. The sheep and vineyards become a distant memory as she revels in palace luxury.

In fact the new queen's love for the king becomes secondary to living a life of luxury. This becomes painfully evident one day as he invites her to go away with him to a secluded place, where he can have her undivided attention and can see her face and hear her voice apart from the distractions of the palace. Unwilling to leave the splendor of the palace for the desolate wilderness camp, she declines his invitation and remains alone at the palace.

Before long, however, the quietness of the palace reveals the growing emotional distance that exists between the Shulamite and the king. She realizes that she has replaced true love's intimacy with the cares of palace life. In the stillness of the night she arises, dresses, and hits the streets to look for her beloved king. Soon the watchmen find her, but they cannot help her locate him. As she continues her search, he suddenly appears out of nowhere. Overcome with joy and relief, she takes him to the nearby home of her mother.

What a sweet time of renewal this husband and wife share together! After he removes her veil, his eyes travel from the top of her head to the tips of her toes. Never has she felt so vulnerable or, oddly, so secure as when she stands before him. After closely inspecting her body he begins a running commentary on what he sees. Speaking softly he describes her appearance as fair and her eyes as those of a dove. He describes her hair, teeth, lips, mouth, forehead, neck, and breasts. He ends his description by saying, *"You have ravished my heart . . . Your love is better than wine."* What joy, what intimacy they share! After a brief second honeymoon they return to palace life.

Before long, however, their lives and their intimacy again become routine. Once more, palace life consumes the Shulamite's attention, until one evening the king knocks at her door. She denies his entrance with the excuse that she already is in bed, that she already has removed her robe, and that she does not want to get her feet dirty. In other words she has a headache! Rejected, he quietly leaves.

Seconds pass into minutes. The following desolate quiet confronts the Shulamite's stubborn resistance. Goaded into action, she yanks open the door and searches for her husband. Nowhere to be found—he is gone. She calls him, but he doesn't answer. The city streets beckon her; the watchmen find her. They beat her and take away her veil. Horrified but resolute, she continues her search. She knocks on the doors of her friends, the daughters of Jerusalem. They have not seen her Beloved. "Give up looking for him," they cry, "What kind of love would allow you to be beaten by the very ones who are there to protect you? Why wasn't he there for you? Forget him!"

Quickly the Shulamite springs to the king's defense. She begins by describing him as *handsome*—one in ten thousand. She describes his hair, eyes, cheeks, lips, hands, body, legs, and mouth. She summarizes her description by declaring, "*He is altogether lovely; he is my lover and my friend.*"

"Wow!" say the city girls. Impressed by her endearing description—despite her recent beating by the watchmen—they join her in her search. Locating his garden, they find him. Rejoicing, the Shulamite woman and the king renew their love. After inspecting her from toe to head, he affirms her by describing her feet as lovely in sandals, her thighs like jewels, her navel and her waist as a heap of wheat, her two breasts as fawns. Her neck is like a palm tree. His eyes and voice travel over her eyes, nose, head, and hair. No reproofs or unkind words has he for her. Moved by his affirmation she simply declares, "*I am my Beloved's and his desire is toward me.*"

Over time this awkward, immature shepherd girl becomes a woman of strength, character, and influence. Everyone who encounters her is amazed by the transforming power of the king's love. Enchantment with the king has finally replaced the pleasures of the palace. Together they go forth into his fields, villages, and vineyards. And they live happily ever after.

Chapter 1

What Women Want

In a recent comedy film titled *What Women Want*, actor Mel Gibson portrays a man who understands what women really want in a man. His character is a sensitive mind-reader who anticipates and moves to meet every need of the woman in his life. *Our longings give us away.* To love and be perfectly loved is the desire of every woman. The Shulamite woman expresses this desire intensely. With almost feverish energy the Song begins with the Shulamite describing her longing for the king's kisses and embrace. His scent and the utterance of his name give her the shivers. She is not alone in her desire. Other women long for this kind of love.

Love's longings (1:1-3)

The Shulamite:
"Let him kiss me with the kisses of his mouth—
For your love is better than wine.
Because of the fragrance of your good ointments,
Your name is ointment poured forth;
Therefore the virgins love you.
Draw me away!"

The daughters of Jerusalem:
"We will run after you."

Incredibly, the king has chosen from among other women the Shulamite, this young Israelite woman from the tribe of Ephraim and a keeper of the vineyard (1:6). She is much like Cinderella with her stepsisters. She is from a blended family. Her mother has two sons (perhaps from an earlier relationship). This gives the Shulamite two half-brothers or stepbrothers and at least two younger sisters. Her father is not mentioned; apparently he is absent. That her brothers do not appreciate her is apparent by their demand that she prune the vines, set traps for the little foxes that spoil the vines, and care for the flock. She works such long hours that she has no time to care for herself. Daydreaming colors her day.

She dreams of an exclusive love relationship with the most powerful and unlikely person to give it—the king. Yes, our longings do give us away. Knowing what our longings are and experiencing them deeply is important. The person not in touch with his or her longings will not be drawn to the source of their satisfaction.[1] Each of us needs a significant individual in our life to love and accept us.

Love's initiation (1:4)

A world of differences separates the shepherd girl and the king; access to his world is improbable and impossible. Her dreams become reality; the inconceivable happens. Her mind is blown away when that handsome, altogether adorable, desirable King extends his love to her.

The Shulamite:
"The King has brought me into his chambers"

The King's chamber: the place of intimacy

The word, *chamber (heder)*, means "compartment or room (within a building) which affords privacy. It is the bedroom of the king, ruler, or bridegroom."[2] Like a womb to a developing baby, what goes on in the private chamber determines the strength of the relationship in the outside world. The bedroom or inner chamber of the marriage is a place of engagement, exclusion, and exploration and enjoyment.

Engagement: Living in shared space forces communication, encourages selflessness, and offers great challenge. Time together is necessary to get to know each other, to appreciate each other's differences, to learn to complement each other's strengths and weaknesses.

Exclusion: Though the marriage relationship fuses together two extended families, the bedroom is no place to include others.

Exploration and enjoyment: The marriage ceremony joins together two lives; the bedroom consummates the union and offers opportunity for partners to learn to please not themselves but the other person.

Love's spectators (1:4d, e)

The daughters of Jerusalem:
"We will be glad and rejoice in you.
We will remember your love more than wine."

Like an intoxicating wine the Shulamite's love rouses the pleasure and applause of her friends; they are amazed and pleased by his selection and rejoice with her in her good fortune. The woman at the well beautifully illustrates this; after her encounter with the Living Water she returns to the city and testifies of the One who meets the deepest longing of the soul. Immediately the townspeople respond by placing their hope in the Lord Jesus.

Love's inadequacy (1:4f-11)

The Shulamite:
"Rightly do they love you.
I am dark, but lovely,
O daughters of Jerusalem,
Like the tents of Kedar,
Like the curtains of Solomon.
Do not look upon me, because I am dark,
Because the sun has tanned me.
My mother's sons were angry with me;
They made me the keeper of the vineyards,
But my own vineyard I have not kept."

No wonder she logs so many frequent-flyer miles; every day she takes flights of fantasy. Imagine a king falling in love with her and taking her away from the strenuous work and difficult home situation! Not a chance. She is a simple shepherd girl. Her hands are rough and calloused. The tip of her nose has a perpetual peel from daily exposure to the sun. She is insecure about her appearance; she is self-conscious and even apologetic about it.

The Shulamite compares herself unfavorably with the daughters of Jerusalem. Certainly they have what is necessary to attract a king. The town-girls are manicured, pedicured, and groomed for marrying such a king. Waited on hand and foot by servants they have time to primp and be pampered. *"Rightly do they love you."* Certainly he is more suited to a city girl.

Aware of the difference the hardships of life have made on her appearance, she supposes she is ugly in comparison to the city girls and therefore disqualified to be noticed by a king.

Oh, the dreams she dreams! I imagine she is no different from today's young women the world over who dream over magazine photos of England's Prince William and Prince Harry. Only one Prince William is to be had; millions of girls hope they will be the one he chooses as his princess. Of course he will choose the stunningly beautiful and rich. Women of every generation have their own dream man. I suppose the women of my generation dream of men like Pierce Brosnan and Tom Cruise.

Women who are groomed to marry kings are not found in shepherds' fields. Compared to the Jerusalem city girls the Shulamite will never be able to catch the king's eye. Princess candidates are found in the city. Kings rarely spend time away from the palace or the capital city; they certainly are not found in the fields. Only dreamers are found in shepherd's fields and vineyards.

A vineyard has to be tended. The Shulamite cultivates the vineyards of her family by digging and removing stones (of which Israel has more than its share. I have heard people say that at creation God had two bags of rocks—one He shook over the world and the other He dumped on the Middle East). Grape shoots need to be planted, watered, and weeded.

After the vineyard becomes established, pruning will become necessary. A vineyard-keeper and shepherd's work is never done. For protection hedges and walls are built around the vineyard. A tower is constructed for storage and for watching over the vineyard. No white-collar laborer is she but a manual laborer—a field hand. She bears the physical results of arduous work and is only too aware that she is different from the city girls.

Today's top-10 fiction lists nearly always include romance novels. Women want romance. They want to be wooed and pursued but not just by any man. They want to be found desirable by the most wanted, celebrated bachelor who is rich, handsome, mysterious, unselfish, manly, strong, and sexual—perfect. The bad news—no such man exists. And, even if he does exist, he does not want me or you. Publicity may enhance the self-esteem of those who associate with royalty, while those of lower class often feel envious and devalued by their exclusion.

To escape the mundane and lonely existence of unmet longings, many women collect large numbers of frequent-flyer miles traveling lengthy flights of fantasy into a make-believe world, where perfect love is poured out on the anonymous, average woman with whom they can identify. We are only too aware of our inadequacies and inabilities to attract perfect love. We long to be included and accepted, not kept outside or distant by our lack of superior looks, breeding, or education.

(To her beloved):
"Tell me, O you whom I love,
Where you feed your flock,
Where you make it rest at noon.
For why should I be as one who veils herself
By the flocks of your companions?"

She seeks to be near him constantly and pleads, *"Tell me . . . where you feed your flock, where you make it rest at noon."* During the early phase of most relationships one or both partners struggle with insecurity. Insecure, the Shulamite fears that the Beloved is ashamed of her. Concerned, she suggests she be veiled so he is protected from the scorn of others by his choice of one so unlikely.

Insecurity drives women to do the strangest things to cover their fears and vulnerabilities. "The real 'us' is masked by our external appearance, and we feel the stare might penetrate behind that mask and threaten us at the deepest level of our being . . .. We feel disrobed, defenseless and naked . . .. She is not at ease with herself."[3]

Love's declaration (1:8-11)

After the Shulamite's initial confession in chapter one about her seemingly disqualifying flaws of discoloration and family dysfunction, she never brings them up again in the Song. Why is that?

The Beloved:
"If you do not know, O fairest among women,
Follow in the footsteps of the flock,
And feed your little goats
Beside the shepherds' tents.
I have compared you, my love,
To my filly among Pharaoh's chariots.
Your cheeks are lovely with ornaments,
Your neck with chains of gold."

Wow! "*O, fairest among women.*" Comparing herself unfavorably with the daughters of Jerusalem, the Shulamite falls short, but the Beloved tells her that she's the fairest among women. What has changed? *Absolutely nothing!* She is exactly the same as she had always been—no plastic surgery, no skin-lightening cream, no trips to the day spa—no tightening and whitening, no buffing and toning. Unlike Cinderella, no magic wand is waved over her to transform her into something she is not. Family history is not re-written to replace her family with a "Leave-It-to-Beaver" family. Nothing external changes! An internal change, however, takes place as she sees herself through his eyes.

Powerful words are spoken to her by the Beloved. Spoken by a lesser, these same words would not pack such a punch. Originating from a king, they are revolutionary.

The Beloved compares her to his filly among Pharaoh's chariots. This sounds demeaning to the sensitivities of the women of our generation, but it is no slight to the Shulamite woman and the women of her day. Stallions, not mares, are used to pull chariots in antiquity. A mare, therefore, among the stallion-driven chariots might well start chaos. The point of comparison is that, in Solomon's opinion, she is as beautiful and sought-after as if she is the only woman in a world full of men.[4] She is in a category all her own with no competitors.

This reminds me of a story told in Africa about the nine-cow wife. In Africa a *lobola* (a bride's price) is given to the woman's family by the groom's family in remuneration for the loss of service provided to her family. The typical price is several cows, a few goats, perhaps some chickens, and a set sum of money. The *lobola* works like insurance. Should the daughter become a widow and return to her family, the family will have the means to support her. This story is about an unattractive yet diligently working woman whom the family is unable to marry off.

One day a young man's family offers nine cows for this scrawny young woman. Her family negotiates down, "Why she is not worth more than a goat or two," they say. A nine-cow offering is like offering a million dollars for a plow horse, when a million dollars easily could buy a beautiful race horse. At the young man's insistence, his family obstinately offers nine cows for the young woman. The deal is struck and the bride's family members are amazed at their good fortune (they easily would have settled for one goat as the exchange). After the marriage celebration she packs up her belongings and becomes a part of the groom's family.

Several years later former villagers and family visit the young woman. They are amazed at the transformation that has taken place during the interim. She absolutely glows with happiness. Marriage obviously agrees with her. She knows she is not worth nine cows, her family knows she is not worth nine cows. The price paid for her changes her entire perspective. She begins to live up to the price paid for her. She becomes a nine-cow woman!

More and more women grow up in dysfunctional families. They hear lies about themselves. This results in a distorted understanding of who they are. Much of their adulthood is defined by the pains and hurts of the past. Though the past cannot be undone, it can be seen from a different perspective—from God's perspective. For women to discover who they are in Christ is important! They are forgiven, accepted, qualified, gifted, and blessed.

The daughters of Jerusalem:
*"We will make you ornaments of gold
With studs of silver."*

Well-meaning friends are these companions. To accessorize her plain looks, they offer to make her jewelry. Imagine her pre-wedding jitters! All of her friends want to be a part of her special day. *Let me do your hair. You need a facial and your nails need a French manicure. How about false eyelashes? Wear these pearls. These earrings look better.* Then imagine her frustration as she listens to all of those suggestions. She is chosen in her natural state; no alterations or improvements are necessary. He loves and accepts her as she is.

Love's fulfillment (1:12-14)

The Shulamite:
*"While the king is at his table,
My spikenard sends forth its fragrance.
A bundle of myrrh is my beloved to me,
That lies all night between my breasts.
My beloved is to me a cluster of henna blooms
In the vineyards of En Gedi."*

Her thoughts, no longer on her lack of qualifications, are captivated by his love. Like the nine-cow wife, she absolutely glows. Her dream is now reality.

Warmed by body heat, the aroma of the myrrh (in a sachet worn around her neck) continually reminds the Shulamite of her Beloved as each scent of pleasure explodes in her nostrils. Her Beloved is a beautiful cluster of henna blooms—fragrant and sweet—not only relished with the eye and worn close to the heart but enjoyed with all the senses.

Love's mutual affirmation (1:15-17)
The Beloved:
"Behold, you are fair, my love!

Behold, you are fair!
You have dove's eyes."

The psychological effects of praise and affirmation are beneficial to the Shulamite's well-being. Given unconditional love and acceptance she exudes joy; the bud of hope has blossomed into a glorious flower. No longer is the Shulamite woman wrapped up in her insecurities. She is loved! He rocks her world. In antiquity, doves are noted for their cleanliness and tranquility. "According to Rabbinic teaching, a bride who has beautiful eyes possesses a beautiful character; they are an index to her character."[5] Her eyes reflect the peace his love has produced.

Sitting on my lap, looking intensely into my eyes, my daughter at 2-years old said, "Mommy, I see little Jennifer in your eyes." Of course she did. I saw myself in her eyes in the same way she saw her own reflection in my eyes. Jesus urges believers to be wise as serpents but as gentle as doves— trusting and peaceful birds. The Beloved's love strikes a responsive chord in her heart. Her eyes simply reflect that trust.

The Shulamite:
"Behold, you are handsome, my beloved!
Yes, pleasant!
Also our bed is green.
The beams of our houses are cedar,
And our rafters of fir."

This is the first of many times in the Song that the Shulamite refers to the Beloved as her lover—her beloved. I find I love most those who unconditionally accept me. Don't you? Not only has she undergone an internal makeover, but even her surroundings are noticeably different. No longer is

she the dreamer of the sheepfold but the dweller of an outdoors love nest, with dew lying on the lush grass and over-
shadowed by a canopy of lush and fragrant tree limbs.

Four truths
We can learn four truths from the Shulamite's initial struggle with poor self-esteem.

**1. Your flaws do not disqualify you from intimacy with
the Beloved King.** I don't know about you, but because I have
teen-aged children, my daily table is not set with my special
crystal and silver. I use inexpensive and easily replaced dishes
and plastic glasses. Entrees are served in common glassware.
The fancy stuff is pulled out of the china cabinet at Easter,
Thanksgiving, and Christmas. Crystal is fragile. It chips easily
and is impractical for daily use. Even storage is a problem, as
crystal cannot be stored in the heat of an attic. My fancy china
can't be washed in the dishwasher. The silver is high-
maintenance; it needs frequent polishing to keep its shine. It is
all pretty to use, but it is impractical in a household filled with
young adults. Only with gentle nudging does my family notice
the special setting; their interests lie in what the dishes contain.

Dishes neither add nor take away the food's flavor or nutritional value. When my mother-in-law was living, I enjoyed
watching her make cornbread dressing. She mixed it in a huge
Tupperware bowl that sported a large, conspicuous bubble on
its side. Years earlier stove-top heat had created the bubble.
Not for one moment did the unsightly bubble diminish the
taste or consistency of the dressing. Its usage had little to do
with aesthetics but with its ability to contain the dressing.

**God's selection criteria are radically different from
those of people.** God does not first make us perfect and then

accept us on that basis.[6] He accepts us, flaws and all—fully and completely in Christ Jesus. He then begins the lifelong process of perfecting us. That process finally will culminate in heaven. People are the ones who discriminate based on appearance. Israel is thrilled with its first king, Saul, who is chosen for his size and appealing appearance but who has little internal character and is a failure. David, unfavorably compared to all of his older brothers, though imperfect, is a man after God's own heart—and the better king.

Four women mentioned in the genealogy of Jesus Christ have something in common: they all are flawed. Though dissimilar in their impairments, they are connected by their inclusion in the lineage of Jesus.

Tamar understands rejection. She marries one of Judah's sons, who later dies before they have any children. Dictated by the custom of that day of perpetuating the lineage, Judah promises another of his sons to her but later refuses to fulfill his promise to her. So she dresses as a harlot and goes undercover to deceive and have a child by Judah. And conceive she does—twins.

You remember **Rahab**. She understands what having a past means. Of the eight times the Bible mentions her, only in the genealogy of Christ is her description—*the harlot*—deleted. Otherwise, she always is defined as *the harlot*. How would you like *the harlot* as your last name? Not only is she a harlot, she is a pagan—an idol worshiper. I wonder what drove her to harlotry. Perhaps abused as a child, she sees having sex as a means of feeling loved. Or maybe she has aging family; prostitution is the only way a single woman can support her family. Who knows how she fell into this dishonorable trade? I am fairly confident that she, as a young girl, did not decide to make harlotry her life ambition. At the demolition of Jericho she and her family are spared death because of her faith in

God demonstrated by the hiding of the spies. Her son, Boaz, is a great-grandfather of King David.

Boaz marries **Ruth**, a Canaanite widow woman. Ruth knows what feeling alone—her life turned upside-down with nowhere to go—is like. Through the influence of her former mother-in-law (never underestimate your influence in the life of your daughter-in-law), she renounces idol worship and follows the God of Israel. King David is her great-grandson.

King David commits adultery with **Bathsheba,** another man's wife. She becomes pregnant with his child. He then has her husband killed and marries her. In the genealogy she simply is described as the one who had been Uriah's wife. She is not even mentioned by name. Bathsheba is a woman who understands shame and heartache. Their first son dies; their second son is King Solomon, the writer of the Song of Solomon and an ancestor of Jesus Christ.

Though flawed each woman becomes a significant spiritual contributor to the genealogy of Christ. The following story posted on the Internet punctuates this truth.

A waterbearer in India had two large pots. Each hung on each end of a pole which he carried across his neck. One of the pots had a crack in it. The other pot was perfect and always delivered a full portion of water at the end of the long walk from the stream to the master's house, while the cracked pot arrived only half-full. Every day for two full years this went on, with the bearer delivering only one-and-a-half pots full of water to his master's house.

Of course the perfect pot was proud of its own accomplishment—perfect to the end for which it was made. But the poor, cracked pot was ashamed of its own imperfection and miserable that it was able to accomplish only half of what it had been made to do.

One day after two years of what it perceived to be a bitter failure, by the stream it spoke to the waterbearer, "I am ashamed of myself, and I want to apologize to you." "Why?" asked the potbearer, "What are you ashamed of?" "For the past two years I have been able to deliver only half my load. This crack in my side causes half of the water to leak out all the way back to your master's house. Because of my flaw, you have to do all this work. You don't get full value from your efforts," answered the cracked pot. The waterbearer felt sorry for the poor cracked pot. In his compassion he said, "As we return to the master's house, I want you to notice the beautiful flowers along the path."

Indeed, as they went up the hill, the cracked pot took notice of the sun warming the beautiful wildflowers on the side of the path. This cheered it some. But at the end of the trail, it still felt badly because it had leaked out half its load. Again the pot apologized to the bearer for its failure.

The bearer said to the pot, "Did you notice that there were flowers only on your side of the path, but not on the other pot's side? That's because I have always known about your flaw, and I took advantage of it. I planted flower seeds on your side of the path, and every day while we walked back from the stream, you have watered them. For two years I have been able to pick these beautiful flowers to decorate my master's table. Without you being just the way you are, he would not have this beauty to grace his house."[7]

Each of us has his or her own unique flaws. In some way we all are cracked pots. But if we allow it, the Lord will use our flaws to grace His Father's table.

In God's great economy, nothing goes to waste—even flaws. These women are included in Jesus' genealogy to display God's grace through their flawed and cracked lives. Water spilled on the path of history through the lives of many flawed individuals has produced the most beautiful flowers for the Master's table. The past, repented of and seen from God's perspective, really is a stepping stone to a deeper relationship with the Beloved.

2. Desiring unconditional love is not wrong. We are designed to enjoy relationships. However human relationships are limited in their ability to provide the unconditional love for which we so desperately long. The Shulamite's longings cannot be quenched by any other, any lesser than the Beloved; they only can be satisfied truly by the King. Human relationships cannot meet the deepest longing for love and acceptance. When we expect too much from others, we are disappointed; our longings for intimacy are unfulfilled. Many relationships are fractured by both those consumed by their flaws and those who demand perfection from their partners. Only God knows all about us and loves us as we are.

My childhood was a painful one. I grew up with a dad who was a hot-tempered alcoholic and compulsive gambler. We moved more times than I can remember. My mother was the glue that held our family together. Over the years the violence increased. Eventually it became so bad that she feared for her life and sought police protection. When they finally divorced, I had been living in Israel for nearly a year (I was 20 years old). Unable to return to the U.S. to comfort my mom and be comforted, I had to deal with the pain alone. One morning during my devotional time with the Lord, through Psalm 45:10-11

God responded to my hurt.

> *Listen, O daughter, consider and incline your ear;*
> *Forget your own people also and your father's house;*
> *So the King will greatly desire your beauty;*
> *Because He is your Lord, worship Him.*

Those words were music to my aching heart. My Beloved Father invited me near. I felt His embrace and heard Him whisper, "I am your Father; you are beautiful to me. I hear and bear your pain. I love you." Weeping as I type, I recall that sweet and powerful moment as a 20-year old *Shulamite woman* who longed for and received tender love from a king. My daddy never told me I was beautiful nor affirmed me. And I am glad. Otherwise I would not fully have appreciated those glorious words spoken to me by my Heavenly Beloved.

The fact that I am, at best, average-looking does not matter to my Heavenly Beloved. The moon has no light or beauty of its own; it merely reflects the light and beauty of the sun. Paul describes this best,

> *But we all, with unveiled face beholding as in a mirror*
> *the glory of the Lord, are being transformed into the*
> *same image from glory to glory, just as by the Spirit of*
> *the Lord* (2 Cor. 3:18).

The word *glory* can mean *appearance.* "God's opinion marks the true value of things, as they appear to the eternal mind, and God's favorable opinion is true glory."[8]

The more I look at Him and He looks at me, the more my countenance shines and I radiate His beauty, regardless of my age at the time. The Psalmist describes this glory,

There are many who say, "Who will show us any
good?" Lord, lift up the light of Your countenance
upon us (Ps. 4:6).

The Shulamite is changed "from glory to glory" as she
interacts intimately with the Beloved.

A popular song speaks of looking for love in all the wrong
places. Many women look for love in all the wrong places.
Even women in strong Christian marriages long for and expect
a kind of love that husbands are unable to give. I like the sub-
title of Gary Thomas's excellent book, *Sacred Marriage: What
if God designed marriage to make us holy more than to make
us happy?* My husband, Stan, is totally awesome. As wonderful as he is, though, he cannot totally meet my deepest longings for affirmation and affection. Certainly God uses him to
demonstrate His love to me, but he cannot fill the place that
only God is able to fill. I am Shepherd-shaped. I am made to
know and experience intimacy with God.

**Our flaws heighten our awareness of our Shepherd-
shaped vacuum.** Paul expresses the God-love for which we so
deeply long:

*But because of his great love for us, God, who is rich
in mercy, made us alive with Christ even when we were
dead in transgressions—it is by grace you have been
saved. And God raised us up with Christ and seated us
with him in the heavenly realms in Christ Jesus, in
order that in the coming ages he might show the
incomparable riches of His grace, expressed in his
kindness to us in Christ Jesus. For it is by grace you
have been saved, through faith—and this is not from
yourselves, it is the gift of God—not of works, so that
no one can boast. For we are God's workmanship,*

created in Christ Jesus to do good works, which God prepared in advance for us to do.[9]

Flaws do not disqualify us as potential recipients of God's love; they magnify the love of God that has been poured out on us through the atoning death of His Son. *Dead in transgressions*—not a very desirable state in which to be found. In Romans chapter five we are described as *enemies, sinners, without strength, ungodly.* Paul emphasizes that, while flawed by sin,

God demonstrated His own love toward us, in that while we were still sinners, Christ died for us (Rom. 5:8).

The verse ends with the price God paid to demonstrate His love: the death of His Son. Recognizing our flaws is the first step to receiving God's gift of grace.

When I was a child, I was deeply afraid of my dad. I hid under my bed when I heard the gravel crunch under the tires of his car announcing his arrival home from work or wherever he had been. Timidity and fear shaped me into an insecure loner. Even after a dramatic salvation experience as a 16-year-old, I still was timid and extremely insecure. Crippled emotionally by my dad's anger and rejection, I struggled with intense anxiety and feelings of abandonment.

These fearful feelings seeped over into my spiritual life. I began to doubt my salvation experience, though it had been dramatic. I spent many months—even years—riding the roller-coaster highs of assurance and lows of intense doubt. If praying a sinner's prayer saves a person, then I was the most saved person on earth. I constantly scrutinized my salvation experience to make sure that I had "done it correctly." Peace eluded me. These feelings of insecurity, rejection, and abandonment held captive my spiritual life. Finally the words of Colossians 1:12-14 penetrated my heart and brought me freedom.

Giving thanks to the Father who has qualified *us to be partakers of the inheritance of the saints in the light. He has* delivered *us from the power of darkness and* conveyed *us into the kingdom of the Son of His love, in whom we have redemption through His blood, the forgiveness of sins.* (Emphasis is mine.)

Qualified stems from the word *hikanotes,* which means "able, sufficient." It is better understood by its antonym, which means "a falling short."[10] I am insufficient. I do fall short. The Father, however, qualifies me. Through the substitutionary death of His Son, Jesus Christ, on the cross, I have peace with God. Jesus is the means by which I am presentable to the Father. I retrain my emotions to respond to God's truth instead of reacting by habit, as I did in the past, to hurt and rejection from my dad. I keep relating to God by faith in Jesus Christ while my feelings mature and respond to God's truth about my status with Him.

Delivered stems from the word *rhuomai,* which means "to draw or snatch from danger, to loose, rescue."[11] It involves more than rescuing from someone or something (domain of darkness). It is the rescue *from* something (darkness) to someone or something else (light). In my rescue I am not lifted out but then deserted or forsaken there at the spot of delivery. People are often delivered from death in a car wreck only to die at the hospital. That is not the kind of deliverance of which Paul speaks. It is a rescue from danger and death to peace and life.

Conveyed is from the word *methistano* and means "a change or place or condition."[12] It describes the completion of

God's deliverance. My domain was darkness, but I have been transferred into His kingdom of light. He is the One who makes the transaction; I am not. I have been acted on. I do not deliver myself; I am helpless to do so. He delivers me. He transfers me into His family and out of that horrible darkness. The words of a Squire Parsons song immediately spring to mind, "I could not come to where He was, so He came to me." As I face my trust issues and fears and believe the Word of God, over time my fickle feelings are overcome by what the Bible says is true about me.

What about you? Are you expecting your husband, another man, or a family member, to give you unconditional love? When he is unable to do so, do you become angry and resentful and punish him in a multitude of small ways? Admit that these persons, in their limitations, cannot give you that for which you long .

Draw near to God and He will draw near to you
(Jas. 4:8).

Ask the Beloved to show you the kind of intimacy and acceptance He offers.

Interpersonal relationships within the body of Christ are revitalized as we grasp the truth Paul abbreviates when he says,

Having predestined us to adoption as sons by Jesus Christ to Himself, according to the good pleasure of His will to the praise of the glory of His grace, by which He has made us accepted in the Beloved (Eph. 1:5-6).

In the same way that I am accepted in the Beloved, so, too, are other believers accepted in Him. I would do well to remember that!

3. Eventually words of affirmation outnumber and outweigh negative thoughts. What we think does matter! True transformation takes place when we have a renewed mind (Rom. 12:2). **We live up to what we believe about ourselves.**

Do not eat the bread of a miser, nor desire his delicacies; for as he thinks in his heart, so is he. Eat and drink! he says to you, but his heart is not with you (Prov. 23:6-7).

A miser is a rich man who lives and acts as though he is a man in poverty. Though he has plenty to give, he resents anyone who takes him up on his offer. He is stingy. He believes that if he shares his resources, he will soon run out. The miser is held captive by his own stinginess. God surfaces and confronts lies I believe; as I face the truth, He sets me free. The Beloved confronts the Shulamite's belief system, communicates his truth to her, and sets her free.

Take a few minutes to read out loud the entire Song of Solomon. Follow the list of all the incredible things the Beloved says about her.

Throughout the Song he describes the Shulamite woman as:

- *"Fairest among women"*
- Lovely in cheeks and neck
- *"Fair, my love"*
- Dove-eyed
- Like *"a lily among thorns"* so is my love among the daughters

And, he invites her to:
- *"Rise up, my love, my fair one, and come away"*
- *"O my dove . . . let me see your face"*
- *"Let me hear your voice; for your voice is sweet and your face is lovely"*

Again, he affirms:
- *"You are fair, my love! Behold, you are fair!"*
- *"Your teeth are like a flock of shorn sheep"*
- *"Your lips are like a strand of scarlet"*
- *"Your mouth is lovely"*
- *"Your temples behind your veil are like a piece of pomegranate"*
- *"Your neck is like the tower of David"*
- *"Your two breasts are like two fawns"*
- *"You are all fair, my love"*
- *"There is no spot in you"*
- *"Come with me from Lebanon, my spouse"*
- *"How fair is your love, my sister, my spouse"*
- *"The fragrance of your garments is like the fragrance of Lebanon"*
- *"O my love, you are as beautiful as Tirzah, lovely as Jerusalem, awesome as an army"*
- *"Your eyes overcome me"*
- *"Your hair is like a flock of goats"*
- *"Your teeth are like a flock of sheep"*
- *"My dove, my perfect one, is the only one"*
- *"Fair as the moon"*
- *"Clear as the sun"*
- *"Awesome as an army with banners"*
- *"How beautiful are your feet in sandals, O prince's daughter"*
- *"The curves of your thighs are like jewels"*

- *"Your navel is a rounded goblet"*
- *"Your waist is a heap of wheat set about with lilies"*
- *"Your neck is like an ivory tower"*
- *"Your eyes are like the pools of Heshbon*
- *"Your nose is like the tower of Lebanon"*
- *"Your head crowns you like Mount Carmel"*
- *"The hair of your head is like purple"*
- *"How fair and pleasant you are, O love, with your delights"*
- *"This stature of yours is like a palm tree"*
- *"And your breasts like its clusters"*
- *"The fragrance of your breath is like apples"*
- *"The roof of your mouth is like the best wine"*

Are you blushing? Enough already, the Shulamite embarrassingly says (pretty heavy stuff!). Then in chapter two she declares, *"I am the rose of Sharon and the lily of the valley."* This declaration is a far cry from chapter one in which she begs him to look away because of her discoloration. What changed? Nothing externally; internally, however, she became a different young woman. Wouldn't you like to be adored like that? Like her, you, too, would change and declare, *"I am the lily of the valley and the rose of Sharon."*

Waterless wells

Talk-show America pictures the broken cistern that is unable to hold water, prophesied by Jeremiah,

"For My people have committed two evils: They have forsaken the fountain of living waters, and hewn themselves cisterns—broken cisterns that can hold no water" (Jer. 2:13).

I saw and cut out the following from a local newspaper column.

Having analyzed selections of Oprah's Book Club, Cynthia Crossen of *The Wall Street Journal* finds them somewhat simple, containing neither ambiguity nor abstract ideas. "The biggest literacy challenge of some Oprah books is their length." Furthermore, the books "portray the modern world as unrelenting, treacherous, and joyless. . . The citizens of Oprah's world are some of the saddest sacks you'll ever meet. If you believed Oprah's books realistically depicted contemporary life, you would have to kill yourself, especially if you are female."[13]

Many of today's women are desperately unhappy with themselves. They plan their schedule around various TV shows which foster desperation and despair. Feeding on such God-vacuumed stuff is crippling for the woman who has experienced the Christian new birth. **True value and self-worth are found only as we relate properly to God.**

As the perception of God grows dim in America, the resulting materialism and emphasis on the external become settled characteristics of our generation. Women live quiet, desperate, and shallow lives.

Never underestimate the power of TV's influence on self-esteem issues. As a child I loved watching the TV series, *The Flying Nun.* Sally Field was my hero. For some reason I strongly identified with her character. Perhaps I envied her ability to fly above and out of her difficulties. As a young girl I had read somewhere that she wore a size-five shoe. Longing to be like her I bought and tried to wear a size-five shoe. Problem—I wear a size-six shoe! I thought that if only I had the same size foot as Sally, then I would at least capture a tiny piece of significant identity.

Because a famous TV or movie personality endorses a subjective beauty product or measurement, we gullibly spend our money and pursue it. Sometimes this is to our own detriment. The pain of a few months freed me from the foolish notion that beauty occurred only with size-five shoes. Years later while I read *Reader's Digest,* I discovered that Sally Field has been in therapy since she was 17 years old. Now why would I want what she has if what she has keeps her in therapy for years?

Designer label: made by God!

I have a strong personality. Early on in my Christian life I tried to change my personality as I responded to 1 Peter 3:3-4:

> *Do not let your adornment be merely outward—arranging the hair, wearing gold, or putting on fine apparel—rather let it be the hidden person of the heart, with the incorruptible beauty of a gentle and quiet spirit, which is very precious in the sight of God.*

I felt that being forthright, daring, and assertive did not look good on a woman, so I tried my best to be gentle and to have a quiet spirit. It was a losing battle! Peter was not referring to the woman's personality but to a spirit of submission. That gives me hope!

Years ago as my husband and I prepared for missionary service, we took the Myers-Briggs personality assessment instrument. As a result I learned the strengths and struggles that accompany my personality. I was enlightened to discover the positive characteristics of my personality and how God can use me in the body of Christ. Yielded to the Holy Spirit my personality can become useful to the kingdom of God.

Old thought-habits are difficult to break. One day while I kicked myself for being loud and entertaining, I was comforted by the psalmist's words,

> *Your hands have made me and fashioned me; Give me understanding, that I may learn your commandments* (Ps. 119:73).

Fascinated by this verse I focused on the words *made* and *fashioned. Made* emanates from the Hebrew word *asa*, meaning *do or make, to bring forth.* The word *made* is broader in meaning than is the word *create. Asa* connotes primarily the fashioning of the object with little concern for special nuances.[14]

Fashion derives its meaning from *kun*—to set up, render proper. It rarely means simply to bring into being. It is not the idea of fixity or firmness in view but rather of basic formation.[15] God's role in forming the human body is significant. The same word is used in Job 31:15:

> *"Did not He who made me in the womb make them?*
> *Did not the same One fashion us in the womb?"*

Formed by His hands. I am a female human like millions of others. Women share general similarities, but no woman (even identical twins) is exactly like any other woman. He made me and He fashioned me individually.[16] He gave me my own build, color, personality, and other characteristics. Though I am like other women generally, no one is quite like me individually. *Unique and one of a kind*, I am my very own *me.*

God likes me that way. This is where we need to pray the second part of Psalm 119:73:

Give me understanding, that I may learn your
commandments.

I need insight into who I am and how I am to respond to God as He sees me individually.

Note the psalmist's declaration about each of us:

You have formed my inward parts;
You covered me in my mother's womb.
I will praise You, for I am fearfully and wonderfully
*   made;*
Marvelous are Your works, and that my soul knows
*   very well.*
My frame was not hidden from You.
When I was made in secret, and skillfully wrought in
*   the lowest parts of the earth.*
Your eyes saw my substance, being yet unformed.
And in Your book they all were written, the days fash-
*   ioned for me,*
When as yet there were none of them.
How precious also are Your thoughts to me, O God!
How great is the sum of them (Ps. 139:13-17).

We all have stories we can tell of absurd things we have done (like worn shoes that were too small) because we believed a lie about our bodies, our looks, and even about our sexuality. Like the Shulamite woman, we will be changed when we discover and believe all that the Beloved says about us.

At first the Shulamite blames her brothers for her lack of desirability.

My mother's sons were angry with me; they made me the keeper of the vineyards. But my own vineyard I have not kept (1:6).

Many women find admitting that they harbor resentment toward God because He made them a certain way to be difficult. They decline to think of their own particular build, hair, face, size of their feet and hands, moles, acne, birthmarks, and family background as being something God created. We incorrectly think that if God really loves us, He would not have made us as we are or that He would change all that we dislike about ourselves.

Only God knows the countless hours and money women spend on tans, nails, makeup, plastic surgery, hair, clothes, dieting, jewelry, cars, and houses to improve or change what God has given to them. And I am not innocent. I have done the acrylic-nails thing, have collected drawers of useless makeup and skin creams, have had moles removed, etc. Life is frustrating because limits exist to the changes we righteously can make to our physical appearance. We work too much on improving the outside and not enough on the inside.

What aspects of yourself do you dislike? Is it your size and shape? Is it a defining feature? Is it aging? Is it a negative focus, like not becoming like one of your parents? In my early years with the Lord, my focus was on not being like my dad. Because I focused on the negative, I felt constant defeat. As I began focusing on becoming the person God intends me to be, I found joy and peace.

Beneath the surface of low self-esteem (characterized by discontentment, anger, bitterness, and addictive behavior, etc.) is really anger toward God. We blame Him for making us as we are, giving us the family we have, allowing us to experience rejection and abuse from those who should love, accept, and protect us. Yet, these can be marvelous stepping stones that lead to a deeper appreciation of grace and self-acceptance.

4. Low self-esteem is a direct result of having poor God-esteem. Someone once said, "It is spiritual ignorance of God which lies at the foundation of all our distrust of Him and, therefore, of all our doubts and fears." Faith is confidence in the revealed character of God. In the minds of many the roles of the enemy and of God have become blurred or even reversed.

> *"The thief does not come except to steal, and to kill, and to destroy, I have come that they may have life, and that they may have it more abundantly"*
> (John 10:10).

Somewhere along the way we have accused God of stealing, killing, and destroying. We have allowed ourselves to believe that what the enemy offers via the world is for our good. How so?

Many are afraid that if they fully surrender their lives to God, He will send them to some Third-World country without electricity and running water. Out of fear many women refrain from submission in marriage—fear they will lose control of finances, kids, etc. Funny how we trust Him for heaven when we die, but we won't trust Him with our life while we live. With knowledge occurs trust. Perhaps we trust Him too little because we know Him so poorly.

The God we sometimes imagine Him to be is not necessarily the God of the Bible. The turning point occurs when we stop seeking the God we want and start seeking the God who is.[17] The revelation of God to us is determined by our character, not by God's (Ps. 18:25-26). If we are mean, that is how God will appear to us. Because we are corrupt, we have a distorted view of God; therefore we cannot imagine anyone, including God, being perfect in character.

Commenting on having a biblical view of God, one author says:

- It is impossible to keep our moral practices sound and our inward attitudes right while our idea of God is erroneous or inadequate. If we would bring back spiritual power to our lives, we must begin to think of God more nearly as He is.
- What comes to mind when we think about God is the most important thing about us.
- A right conception of God is basic to practical Christian living.
- The essence of idolatry is the entertainment of thoughts about God that are unworthy of Him.
- We do the greatest service to the next generation of Christians by passing on to them an undimmed and undiminished concept of God.
- To be right we must think worthy of God. It is morally imperative that we purge from our minds all ignoble concepts of Deity and let Him be the God in our minds that He is in the Universe [and in the Bible].[18]

Only by spending time in the Word of God and allowing the Holy Spirit to illumine our minds will our view of God become clear and biblical. For now let's see what the Bible says about Him:

1. God cannot lie.
- *That by two immutable things, in which it is impossible for God to lie* (Heb. 6:18).

• *In hope of eternal life which God, who cannot lie, promised before time began* (Titus 1:2).

2. God is infinitely good.
• *You are good and do good* (Ps. 119:68).

3. God will not hurt me.
"For I know the thoughts that I think toward you," says the Lord, "thoughts of peace and not of evil, to give you a future and a hope" (Jer. 29:11).

Luke uses two stories to follow Jesus' instruction on prayer: the friend who visits at midnight to beg bread for his houseguest who has recently arrived and the story of the son asking for bread from his father and the unlikely receiving of a stone instead (Luke 11:5-8, 9-13). Commenting on these verses Oswald Chambers notes that "sometimes God will seem unfriendly; He is not! Sometimes He will seem unfatherly; He is not!" He temporarily withholds His response to teach His disciples persistence. Lack of immediate response from God does not warrant accusations from the pray-er.

4. God will correct those who falsely accuse Him.
"These things you have done, and I kept silent; you thought that I was altogether like you [You imagined me to be like yourself]; But I will rebuke you, and set them in order before your eyes" (Ps. 50:21).

5. God is unlike humanity.
"For My thoughts are not your thoughts, nor are your ways My ways," says the Lord. "For as the heavens are higher than the earth, so are My ways higher than your ways, and My thoughts than your

thoughts" (Isa. 55:8-9).

Throughout history humanity has tried to learn about God by studying humanity. We have it all backward. We learn about God by studying God; by studying God we will understand ourselves. God is not like people. Dietrich Bonhoeffer said, "Satan does not here fill us with the hatred of God, but with the forgetfulness of God." By reading Scripture you can continually refresh your view of God.

6. God is accountable to no one.
"Why do you contend with Him? For He does not give an accounting of any of His words" (Job 33:13).

All the inhabitants of the earth are reputed as nothing; He does according to His will in the army of heaven and among the inhabitants of the earth. No one can restrain His hand or say to Him, "What have you done?" (Dan. 4:35).

7. God knows all of your needs.
"Therefore do not be like them, for your heavenly Father knows the things you have need of before you ask Him" (Matt. 6:8).

8. God is all-powerful.
"Ah, Lord God! Behold, You have made the heavens and the earth by Your great power and outstretched arm. There is nothing too hard for you" (Jer. 32:17, 27).
But Jesus looked at them and said to them, "With men this is impossible, but with God all things are possible" (Matt. 19:26).

Now to Him who is able to do exceedingly abundantly above all that we ask or think, according to the power that works in us (Eph. 3:20).

9. God is beyond our understanding.
Have you not known? Have you not heard? The everlasting God, the Lord, the Creator of the ends of the earth, neither faints nor is weary. His understanding is unsearchable (Isa. 40:28).

Oh, the depth of the riches both of the wisdom and knowledge of God! How unsearchable are His judgments and His ways past finding out! (Rom. 11:33).

10. God is compassionate.
But He, being full of compassion, forgave their iniquity and did not destroy them. Yes, many a time He turned His anger away and did not stir up all His wrath (Ps. 78:38).

11. God is a deliverer.
The Lord is my rock and my fortress and my deliverer; My God, my strength, in whom I will trust; My shield and the horn of my salvation, my stronghold (Ps. 18:2).

12. God forgives sin.
If we confess our sins, He is faithful and just to forgive us our sins and to cleanse us from all unrighteousness (1 John 1:9).

13. God is Holy and expects holiness in His children.
But as He who called you is holy, you also be holy in all your conduct (I Pet. 1:15).

14. God is kind and expects kindness in his children.
"For He is kind to the unthankful and evil. Therefore be merciful, just as your Father also is merciful" (Luke 6:35, 36).

15. God is slow to anger.
The Lord is gracious and full of compassion, slow to anger and great in mercy (Ps. 145:8).

16. God is strong and mighty in battle.
*Who is this King of glory? The Lord strong and mighty, the Lord mighty in battle (*Ps. 24:8).

17. God is the King and rules over all.
But the Lord is the true God; He is the living God and the everlasting King. At His wrath the earth will tremble, and the nations will not be able to endure His indignation (Jer. 10:10).

18. God puts a high value on faith and punishes those who do not believe.
But I want to remind you, though you once knew this, that the Lord, having saved the people out of the land of Egypt, afterward destroyed those who did not believe (Jude 25).

All wrong thoughts of God cast a deep shadow over the heart and mind of the soul that entertains them. All defective views of God's character show up in the life and character of the one marred by them. The result is a life of despair, depression, and delusion. Think right thoughts of God if you would worship Him as He desires to be worshiped, if you would live the life He wishes you to live, and if you would enjoy the peace He has provided through Christ Jesus. We can know God only as Scripture reveals Him. Evaluate your view of God and, finding it insufficient, ask God to give you a greater capacity to know Him.

Chapter 2

My Beloved Is Mine, and I Am His

In the preceding chapter we examined the initial stage of the relationship between the two lovers. We identified with the Shulamite woman as she struggled with the challenge of developing a positive self-identity. We saw this insecure woman, once intimidated by an inferiority complex, transform into a confident, Beloved-assured, **Shepherd-shaped woman.** We identified several timeless truths that apply to today's Christian woman. Every growing relationship demands time spent together in intimacy. Chapter two begins with an intimate exchange between the two lovers.

Love's mutual testimony (2:1)

"I am a rose of Sharon,
a lily of the valleys" (NIV).

The Shulamite modestly likens herself to the rose of Sharon. The Hebrew word for *rose, habasselet*, actually is a *crocus.*[19] This common but fragrant meadow flower grows abundantly, after the rainy season, on the maritime slope north of Joppa—the plain of Sharon. Unlike the American rose this flower is not red and requires no special care. Perhaps the Shulamite merely is repeating what the Beloved has already affirmed in chapter one: he likes her just as she is—a low-maintenance woman. A similar flower is mentioned in the "Song of the Blooming Desert" (Isa. 35). Isaiah prophesies of the future glory of Israel and describes the former wasteland and wilderness as a desert rejoicing in bloom.

It shall blossom abundantly and rejoice.

This heart of hers, a former loveless wilderness, no longer is barren with unmet longings. Like the meadow after spring rains, she flourishes.

The Shulamite compares herself to the lily of the valley. This picture has inspired many songs which describe Jesus as the rose of Sharon and the lily of the valley. These self-descriptive words are not spoken by the Beloved but by the Shulamite. This declaration of hers highlights the inner trans-formation of her heart and mind.

The lily of the valley is one of many flower varieties grow-ing in Palestine. Though it is perhaps the carpet on which the Master walked, this simple flower is selected by Jesus to express His Father's care,

"Consider the lilies, how they grow: they neither toil nor spin; and yet I say to you, even Solomon in all his glory was not arrayed like one of these" (Luke 12:27).

Though the lily is commonplace and not as beautiful as other flowers, Jesus chooses this one to make a point. The lily, dependent on external elements, is unable to add to or take away from its own beauty.

In comparison the Shulamite uses the lily to express her humility. Though she is nothing special in and of herself and, in fact, is common and ordinary, she is singled out from among the common and ordinary. After doing an Internet search I was surprised to discover that literally several thousand varieties of the lily exist.

Her statement presents a stark contrast to the one made in chapter one, in which she beats herself up over her appearance. Nothing is wrong with being a lily—being ordinary. Insecurity is a spiritual problem. **Assurance and confidence laced with humility are byproducts of spiritual growth.**

> *Now this is the confidence that we have in Him, that if we ask anything according to His will, He hears us* (1 John 5:14).

Confidence is a direct result of knowing your position in Christ.[20] Knowing and experiencing the security of the loving and accepting relationship one has with Christ makes one humbly confident. The joy of being accepted fully by the Beloved removes the need for a performance-based response and replaces it with a response motivated by love and gratitude.

The Beloved:
"Like a lily among thorns,
Is my darling among the maidens" (NIV).

Though she must not compare herself unfavorably with others (2 Cor. 10:12), the Beloved continues to compare her favorably with her associates. The Beloved echoes the Shulamite's newfound sense of self-worth by comparing her to the lily among thorns, by singling her out from among the other women, and by elevating as exclusive the love the two share.

Envision your own participation in the Miss America beauty pageant. You are in the lineup with the prettiest and most talented women from all 50 states and Puerto Rico. You, Miss Average American, are chosen winner from among the other contestants. Can you hear the public outcry, the media commentary? Even your own heart fills you with a sense of the absurd. You know that under normal circumstances you could never win. The Shulamite struggles with similar feelings.

Though nothing about the Shulamite's appearance and family background changes, she finds peace as her view of herself changes. In the same way God's peace belongs to those who have confidence in His goodness, even when life is tough and their self-concept is poor. Note that we can, at the same time, experience God's peace and a poor self-image.[21] The peace of God enables you to work through a poor self-image and arrive at a place of self-acceptance, even as you sit among other women whom you consider to be more attractive.

Love's protection (2:3)

The Shulamite, sitting with the daughters of Jerusalem, to their attentive ears proclaims her love and praises her Beloved.

"Like an apple tree among the trees of the forest
Is my lover among the young men.
I delight to sit in his shade,
And his fruit is sweet to my taste" (NIV).

What a pleasant surprise you would have to find, while hiking through the middle of a forest, a beautiful apple tree loaded with ripe fruit! The experience would be all the more pleasant if you had missed a meal or two. This scene captures the spirit of the Shulamite's surprise and delight at being loved by the Beloved. She finds in the shadow of his shade a quiet place of rest. She discovers that he also is her protector. Notice the delight she experiences as she sits beneath his shade.

In Bible days a woman without a protector is one to be pitied. Ruth finds a protector in Boaz,

"The Lord repay your work, and a full reward be given you by the Lord God of Israel, under whose wings you have come for refuge" (Ruth 2:12).

Though she is a foreigner and unlike any of his maidservants, she finds safety and confidence in his resting place. David finds under the shadow of God's wings safety from his enemies.

Keep me as the apple of Your eye; hide me under the shadow of your wings, from the wicked who oppress me, from my deadly enemies who surround me (Ps. 17:8-9).

The wisdom writer expresses his confidence in the Lord by declaring

The name of the Lord is a strong tower; the righteous run to it and are safe (Prov. 18:10, NKJV).

Isaiah acknowledges God's hand as his resting place,

in the shadow of His hand He has hidden me,
and

I have covered you with the shadow of My hand (Isa. 49:2; 51:16).

According to Psalm 91 several benefits are promised to those who abide under the shadow of the Almighty and discover His protection.

- *He will deliver you from the snare of the fowler and the perilous pestilence* (3).
- *His truth shall be your shield and buckle* (4).
- *You shall not be afraid of the terror by night, or the arrow flying by day* (5).
- *You shall not be afraid of the pestilence of the dark nor of the destruction of the daytime* (6).
- *You shall see the reward of the wicked* (8).
- *No evil shall befall you, nor shall any plague come near your dwelling* (10).
- *Angels will be charged to protect you* (11-12).

Jesus is the believer's Protector. When Jesus asks him if he will turn back and quit following like others are doing, with deep passion Peter gravely declares,

"Lord, to whom shall we go? You have the words of eternal life. Also, we have come to believe and know that You are the Christ, the Son of the living God" (John 6:68-69).

Peter demonstrates the security and safety found in Jesus as his Protector.

The cool shadow of this apple tree—beautiful in its allure, unexpected in its forest environment, and fragrant in its fruitful aroma—makes a marvelous retreat for the Shulamite. In the Beloved Lord Jesus, the Eternal Tree of Life, we discover the shade of divine righteousness—God's place of rest and renewal. In lives filled 24 hours a day, seven days a week with increasing activity, sin, brokenness, and heartache His shade invites all who are needy to find rest in Him.

In unexpected places and ways God confirms His love for us and shelters us through the cares and trials of life. He does not remove us from these cares; He shelters us in them. Jesus assures the believer with these words,

> "*These things I have spoken to you that in Me you may have peace. In the world you will have tribulation; but be of good cheer, I have overcome the world*" (John 16:33).

The psalmist, beaten down by constant turmoil, turned to God, his Protector.

> *Whom have I in heaven but You? And there is none upon earth that I desire besides You. My flesh and my heart fail; but God is the strength of my heart and my portion forever* (Ps. 73:25-26).

The gospel of grace lifts women. Everywhere the gospel is proclaimed, women are liberated. Many of the world religions treat women harshly. In some Islamic countries religious leaders forbid women's education and keep them hidden behind closed doors and under heavy garments. Islam permits a husband to have four wives; the man may divorce any one of his wives simply by stating three times his intention to divorce her—she is powerless. Until the mid-to-late 1900s the Hindu practice of *suttee* demanded that the living widow be burned with her husband's corpse. In genuine contrast, the Shulamite experiences true liberation.

His banner and banqueting house (2:4-6)

The Shulamite to the daughters of Jerusalem:
"He has taken me to the banquet hall."

A banquet is an elaborate and sumptuous feast given in honor of a person or in celebration of an achievement. Tables are set with fine china, elaborate floral arrangements, and a smorgasbord of foods and various dishes. Banqueting rooms with their ornate silverware and wealthy guests require proper dress and etiquette. He finds her in the vineyard, they meet again in the countryside, and now she is in his house, experiencing all that palace life has to offer. Do you wonder how she conducts herself that first time? Is she jittery, self-conscious, and intimidated? Perhaps. We all have a first time for everything. Reporting to the daughters after the event, the Shulamite provides them with a detailed description of the night's events. In a style altogether too descriptive for our modern-day comfort, she first mentions his banner of love and then speaks of their intimacy.

Banner of protection

"And his banner over me is love."

In the Old Testament a banner is a pole bearing an identifying flag, ensign, or insignia, to act as a rallying point for the tribes of Israel on their march through the wilderness (Num. 2:2-3). It identifies the band of soldiers and represents victory.

Identification. The banner immediately identifies and separates the different tribes. Like a banner the Beloved's love is easily seen by anyone observing their relationship. It is exclusive. His goodness is for public viewing (See Ps. 31:19-21). Acceptance is based on identification. In the same way I am welcomed into the May family because of my union with Stan, I am accepted into the family of God based on my identification with Jesus Christ (John 1:12; Eph. 1:6). The Shulamite's security springs from whose she is, not from who she is.

Victory. The banner also speaks of conquest. At the end of a battle, when Israel's banner remains high and lifted up, Israel's enemies recognize defeat. Banished to the conquered field is the Shulamite's insecurity. Because she stands victorious under His waving banner of love, her inadequacy and insecurity are defeated.

Banquet of provision

"Strengthen me with raisins,
Refresh me with apples,
For I am faint with love."

Banquets lead to overeating, which leads to upset stomachs. Satiated by the banquet experience the Shulamite boasts to her friends of her guiltless pleasure—her lovesickness. She is full to overflowing. Psalm 45 recites the psalmist's response to the love with which he has been loved by God. This prophetic psalm pictures the Messiah's love for the Bride.

"My heart is overflowing with a good theme;
I recite my composition concerning the King;
My tongue is the pen of a ready writer.
You are fairer than the sons of men;
Grace is poured upon Your lips;
Therefore God has blessed You forever (Ps. 45:1-2).

Why does the psalmist's heart overflow? The subject—the King—is too large for his heart. The King is majestic; Jesus says the rocks will shout and praise the Great Creator if the hearts and mouths of the people remain silent. Praising the King, the Samaritan woman hops, skips, jumps, and shouts all the way home after she meets Jesus at the well. She goes to the well in the heat of the day to avoid all the women who draw water in the cool of the morning. Her five failed marriages (she was a serial wife!) and her present live-in lover make her eager to avoid others. Jesus, on a divine appointment, meets her at the well; He exposes and confronts her immorality, forgives her, and gives her living water. Surely she enters the city a different woman than the one who leaves there alone in the heat of the day! She informs the townspeople,

"He told me all that I ever did. He loves and forgives me" (John 4:39).

She has a heart *overflowing with a good theme*!

The Samaritan woman drinks from the well that never runs dry; she eats from the Tree of Life. Refreshment for the Shulamite is found in the apple—the fruit from the tree that provided her shaded rest. Proverbs 25:11 gives a beautiful description of that piece of fruit:

A word fitly spoken is like apples of gold in settings of silver.

Only Jesus, the Living Word spoken to people's hearts, can satisfy the desires of the heart. Attempts to satisfy the restless desires of the heart (yet another man for the woman at the well) with human relationships may silence the cry but will not quench deep longing made and put there by God.

"His left arm is under my head,
And his right arm embraces me."

The Beloved's embrace involves both head and heart; his love affects both mental and emotional health. Just as houses are grounded to protect them from the destructive force of lightning, so both mind and emotions must be grounded in the love of God. Anxious thoughts and fickle feelings—twin passion crushers—are held in check by truth's embrace.

In Phil. 4:6-7 Paul describes God's care for the believer's heart and mind by instructing the believer to shun anxiety by praying about everything and to concentrate all mental capacities on meditating on the praiseworthy. God promises that His embrace strengthens and stabilizes the believer:

Fear not, for I am with you; be not dismayed, for I am
your God. I will strengthen you, Yes, I will help you. I
will uphold you with My righteous right hand
(Isa. 41:10).

The psalmist describes the Lord as the One who guards us with His shield, surrounds us with His glory, and lifts our heads (Ps. 3:3).

The Holy Spirit has an affinity for a disciplined mind. Paul promises that transformation will take place in the believer's life as he renews his mind (Rom. 12:2). He also commands the believer to be

renewed in the spirit of your mind (Eph. 4:23).

God promises the believer that perfect peace is obtained as his mind is kept on Him (Isa. 26:3).

The Christian life is not all mental (knowledge) or all heart (emotion). Balance is obtained when both head and heart are engaged by humanity and embraced by God. Paul says love (the heart) and knowledge (the mind) are to travel together (1 Cor. 8:10-13; 13:2). Proverbs expresses the same idea,

He who trusts in his own heart is a fool, but whoever walks wisely will be delivered (Prov. 28:26).

Love for God and obedience to His commandments are inseparable (1 John 5:1-3). Jesus specifically equates love with obedience (John 14:15, 23; 15:10). The Pharisees knew the Scripture but loved neither the Son nor the Father. Emotions alone lead astray. Head knowledge alone makes a person self-righteous. Both the Shulamite's heart and mind are held in sweet captivity.

Theologians actually can miss knowing God as they study about Him. Knowing about God and knowing Him are not the same. As a historian I can seek to know everything I can about George Washington, but his death makes actually knowing him impossible. God is alive! Therefore He is to be known by experience. The death and resurrection of Christ make Him knowable. You can have knowledge without intimacy, but having intimacy without knowledge is impossible.

Guarding your passion (2:7)

"Daughters of Jerusalem, I charge you
By the gazelles and by the does of the field,
Do not arouse or awaken love
Until it so desires."

The Shulamite charges the daughters of Jerusalem, "Don't douse cold water on my passion!" A "Do-not-disturb" sign hangs on the knob of her relationship with the Beloved. Well-meaning people distract. Martha involves Jesus in a sibling issue. She is busy with much serving while her sister, Mary, sits at Jesus' feet and hears His Word. Martha wants Jesus to intervene and to make Mary stop listening to Him and help her. To Martha's dismay, Jesus affirms Mary's choice. He hangs an invisible "Do-not-disturb" sign on Mary's passion.

Gazelles and does are easily frightened; they are cautious and quickly bound away at the slightest rustle of a leaf. Great care must be taken to protect love between the lovers. Intense but fragile passion is easily disturbed. "The adjuration is that love should not be disturbed, and therefore it is by the animals that are most lovely and free, which roam through the fields."[22] Dielitzsch comments on these verses, "The adjuration is repeated, 3:5, 8:4, and wherever Shulamite finds herself near her Beloved, as she is here in his arms. What lies nearer, then, than that she should guard against a disturbance of this love-ecstasy, which is like a slumber penetrated by delightful dreams?"[23]

Emotions can run wild; therefore, a sensitive heart must be guarded and grounded in truth. Passion is high-maintenance; for it to be well-maintained it must be aggressively guarded and kept in check. Knowledge alone is cold and distant. Peter addresses the need for both:

to faith virtue, to virtue knowledge, to knowledge self-control, to self-control perseverance, to perseverance godliness, to godliness, brotherly kindness and to brotherly kindness love (2 Pet. 1:5-8).

With these characteristics the believer becomes fruitful in the knowledge of the Lord Jesus Christ.

For the Shulamite to experience the encompassing embrace (that includes both the heart and the head), she has to venture into the unfamiliar territory—the royal palace. Accustomed to shepherd fields and wild vineyards, the change brings both excitement and anxiety.

Adjustments are a necessary part of life. Leave the past behind. For continued growth, enter new doors. I made many adjustments when I married Stan and became a pastor's wife, a daughter-in-law, a mother, a missionary, and a seminary-professor's wife. Further adjustments have to be made as my kids graduate from high school and college, marry, and have children. The truth of His love for me and His providence in my life keep my anxieties and intimidations in check as I transition from one stage into the next.

Good advice

Perhaps one of the most disturbing rustling noises of a woman's emotional life is PMS. Have you noticed how emotionally sensitive you become during your menstrual cycle (or am I alone)? The slightest thing evokes an upset. Make friends with this enemy of yours by grasping this sensitive left hand of emotion with the stabilizing right hand of knowledge. Direct this extra sensitivity into spiritual energy by spending extra time in the Word of God, thus allowing Him to take advantage of this most sensitive time. Over the years as I have maintained journals of my pilgrimage with the Lord, I have noticed a pattern: during PMS time I seem to have greater insight than on other days as I channeled my emotions and sensitivities to the Lord and to Scripture instead of giving in to moodiness.

During this time never skip your devotions. Utilize this sensitivity for spiritual good.

Love's invitation (2:8-14)

Earlier we focused on the Bride's feelings toward the Beloved. She is delighted with the thought of his visits and with the man and woman's mutual enjoyment of each other. Romance is interspersed with moments of intimacy and distance. She anticipates every encounter.

The Shulamite:
"Listen! My lover!
Look! Here he comes,
Leaping across the mountains,
Bounding over the hills."

The Shulamite's eager anticipation is twofold:
The Shulamite focuses all of her attention on watching and waiting for his approach. **First, she hears His voice as He leaps and skips over the mountain and hills.** She has been waiting for that voice—a voice of both passion and power. My dating relationship with Stan consisted of two years of letters and long-distance phone calls while I lived in Israel. My heart danced every time I heard his voice over the phone from thousands of miles away.

Psalm 29:3-9 lists eight attributes of the Lord's voice:
- It is over the waters (Jesus spoke to the sea. Immediately it was calm!)
- It is thunderous.
- It is powerful. (When called by name Lazarus immediately left the cold of death's tomb.)

- It is majestic.
- It breaks the cedars into splinters and makes them skip like a calf.
- It divides the flames of fire. (In the book of Daniel the Word divides the flames to enter and join the three men in the flaming furnace.)
- It shakes the wilderness. (God judges the Israelites severely for their unbelief.)
- It makes the deer give birth and strips the forests bare.

A voice of strength arouses confidence, not fear; therefore, without fear the Shulamite awaits the sound of the Beloved's arrival. Jesus assures His children that His sheep hear His voice (John 10:10). Just as the Shulamite watches and listens in fearless anticipation for the Beloved's voice, we, too, are to watch with anticipation and listen for Our Lord's voice.

Second, she expects a visit from her Beloved. Love knows no barriers. He arrives with perfect ease; no mountains of difficulties and hills of adverse circumstances are too large to slow him down. He is eager to be in her presence.

The Shulamite compares the Beloved to a gazelle or to a young, frisky stag. The Palestinian gazelle, a smaller member of the deer family, is fleet of foot. These reclusive animals run in pairs and mate for life. They require less water than the hart, which drinks copiously at flowing streams.[24] The handsome male arrives softly and seeks to attract his companion. Lovers, whose thoughts and feelings incessantly revolve around each other, are inclined to exaggerate the actions and approaches of the other. The Shulamite's anticipation is apparent by her exaggeration.

I have been privileged to teach many new believers how to develop a devotional life. One woman, Sharon, is most enthusiastic about spending time with the Lord. She told me that she pictures the Lord Jesus sitting at her kitchen table every morning and waiting for her to join Him. That is anticipation!

> *"My lover is like a gazelle or a young stag.*
> *Look! There he stands behind our wall,*
> *Gazing through the windows,*
> *Peering through the lattice."*

The solid, protective wall of the compound is no real barrier to the Beloved. With the agility of a leaping gazelle the Beloved jumps over the barrier and arrives suddenly and unexpectedly at her room's window. Through the lattice his gaze finally lands on her in the room's dim light. When things are quiet and the Lord seems distant, I am often comforted to remember that He knows my address, knows where to find me, and that He is always near even when I am unaware of His presence.

The Beloved's urgent invitation (2:10-13)

> *"My lover spoke and said to me,*
> *'Arise, my darling,*
> *My beautiful one, and come with me.*
> *See! The winter is past;*
> *The rains are over and gone.*
> *Flowers appear on the earth;*
> *The season of singing has come,*
> *The cooing of doves*
> *Is heard in our land.*
> *The fig tree forms its early fruit;*
> *The blossoming vines spread their fragrance.*

Arise, come, my darling;
My beautiful one, come with me.'"

As wintertime closes, rain in Israel falls with less frequency as the land prepares for springtime. Prophesying of an external expression in love which winter has driven indoors, spring announces its arrival. This elaborate description of spring emphasizes the beauty of the setting and describes the youthful joy of their relationship. Flowers burst into appearance and beg to be enjoyed; their flowering vines sweeten the air. Spring stimulates and heightens the senses of sight, sound, taste, and smell as doves coo, trees bear their fresh, tender leaves, and blossoms promise delicious fruit. Love, newly born in youthful hearts, arouses springlike feelings, since everything seems fresh and new.[25] Enticing as the wonders of spring are, the Beloved invites her away from sensual enjoyment found in the spring-refreshed valley and urges her to go to an obscure, rocky place up in the cliffs.

"My dove in the clefts of the rock,
In the hiding places on the mountainside,
Show me your face,
Let me hear your voice;
For your voice is sweet,
And your face is lovely."

A desire to be alone with one's lover is a characteristic of genuine love. That the Beloved is distressed by the Shulamite's diversion of intimacy because of spring's arrival is obvious. Twice he calls,

"Rise up, my love, my fair one, and come away."

Separation and a break, both with the past experiences (winter) and present enjoyments (spring), are required. The former dark one now is the fair one; the former comfortable places of pastureland and vineyards and the present palace life are to be sacrificed for the beckoning rocky cliffs. This dove of his is invited to the dwelling of an eagle—that solitary, high place. Unlike the eagle, the dove is gentle, harmless, and utterly defenseless. The Beloved's presence and protection is promised; therefore, the unknown and difficult are not to be feared.

Those whom Jesus has lured away from the world unto Himself frequently are found in the rugged scenes of life—in situations of trial, affliction, and desolation—alone. Several years ago while my husband and I ministered alongside a pastor in Central Oregon, we had the opportunity to hike to some of the best rock-rappelling cliffs in North America. (We were observers only!) I was amazed to hear the coo of doves in those forlorn, rocky cliffs as I followed their telltale trails of droppings up those cliffs. My former picture of pigeons/doves fluttering innocently on the streets of London (*Mary Poppins*) has been replaced by Oregon's wilderness sightings. The Beloved exalts the glories of spring, yet his invitation isn't to enjoy the fruits of fair weather but to climb the rocky cliffs away from the spring's pleasures. Strange places for intimacy, these cliffs. His invitation does not end with RSVP. Love, once experienced, has no option but to respond to the seemingly uninviting rocky terrain.

Moses, a fugitive from Egypt, leads his flock to the back of the desert to Horeb (so named for its desolation), where in an unparalleled experience God confronts him at a burning bush. No birds are singing and no flowers are growing; he's surrounded by dust and dried shrubs—and God (Ex. 3). At another rocky place, Mt. Sinai, Moses again experiences God. After an exhibit of great thunder, intense lightning, and thick smoke clouds God, in a still, small voice, converses with Moses (Ex. 19:16ff). In both of these occasions God initiates both the venue and the experience. Both places are desolate; yet, clearly the voice of the Lord is heard! God is encountered.

Elijah, too, is no stranger to dangerous cliffs and desolate rocks. There on Mount Horeb's untamed heights sleeps the prophet Elijah, exhausted and on the run from a bad situation. God meets him in the solitude of the cave's damp darkness, carved in the clefts of the rocks. The storm, the wind, the earthquake, and fire cannot drown the calm voice of God in those desolate heights of the mount (1 Kings 19:9-13). God chooses the meeting place and brings his servant there.

The Apostle John's visions occur on the rocky and desolate Isle of Patmos (Rev. 1:9; 21:10). The risen Lord, now glorified, is revealed in splendor. What a time of great awe and intimacy John experiences with the Beloved! He sees things that no one fully will understand until the marriage supper of the Lamb. At the end of John's vision, an angel closes the scene by taking him to the great and high mountain to show him the holy Jerusalem descending out of heaven from God. Secreted away in the clefts of the rock are intimacies known to few.

What is heard in the clefts of the rock is life-changing for each man. Just as Moses, Elijah, John, and many others have responded to the call to desolate places, so, too, must the believer respond to the voice of the Beloved.

Draw near to God and He will draw near to you
(Jas. 4:8).

Never mind if the place is desolate—the better to hear from God! The message will be life-changing for the one willing to meet with Him there in the cleft of the rocks!

The Beloved issues the invitation, yet the Song is silent to her response. Did the Shulamite trade the comfortable, cozy springtime for wild cliffs and crevices? Such intimacies are promised,

"My dove, my tender, timid one, the object of my deepest, most devoted love, let me see your face."

The very face she once had declared *dark* to him is desirable—even lovely; her voice is sweet. His invitation is a withdrawal from the watchful eye of others to time alone with him—to the mount of obscurity and wilderness.

God delights in our nearness. He, too, benefits from this wonderful relationship. Self-absorbed, we are often guilty of treating God as if He exists for us and not the other way around. We read the Bible as though it were all about us, for our blessing. The truth is that we exist to bring Him pleasure. The Bible is about God—not merely about people. God seeks those with whom He can share Himself. The tragedy of the fall is twofold: we lose fellowship with God, and He no longer is able to walk in the cool of the day with us. God, too, lost something in the Garden of Eden.

The difficult crevices of life are times designed by Him and for Him. The invitation to go where He is commands a surrender of my preoccupation with myself, my happiness, and my comfort, to a more noble aspiration of knowing Him, His purposes, and His character. The invitation is God-centered, not self-centered. He delights to see our faces and hear our voices. Have you realized that God delights to hear you? Draw near to Him right now and let Him enjoy your love. Express that love by reading aloud Psalm 42:1.

Love's distractions (2:15)

Her brothers:
"Catch for us the foxes,
The little foxes that ruin the vineyards,
Our vineyards that are in bloom."

Love is stronger than death, but the enjoyment of it is easily lost. In times of refreshing and after periods of intense spiritual concentration, make protective measures against subtle intrusions. Many a good vine is marred and scarred for an entire season by the cunning craftiness and sharp teeth of the little fox. Havoc is wreaked on the tender vines, bark is stripped, and branches are broken. The damage one fox does to the springtime growth of a vineyard can hinder an entire season's harvest. Though the root remains undamaged for another season, the vine will bear no fruit in the present one. A little spray of blossoms easily is capable of producing a nice, full branch of grapes, yet damaged blossoms fade and die. Though not a large animal, a fox is capable of making great mischief in an unprotected and prosperous vineyard.

The little fox represents anything that injures by stealth and cunning. The fox figure in Scripture is often used to represent a crafty individual. Jesus calls King Herod a *fox* (Luke 13:32). In the Roman Empire Herod is a minor official; yet, *this fox* wields considerable influence. He is responsible for the death of at least two major biblical characters: John the Baptist and James the brother of John.

In order to bear fruit that lasts, believers must jealously guard the vine. Unless the little foxes are kept at bay, barrenness will characterize the believer's life. The believer is responsible for abiding in the vine (John 15:5). No fruit-bearing occurs in the life of the one not abiding in Jesus. God is glorified by the abundance of fruit born by His disciples (John 15:8). Many times the little things in our lives do the most damage. The Bible mentions two categories of little things:

Positive *little* things:
A *little* coin, once lost but now recovered, brings rejoicing (Luke 15:9).
A *little* touch on the hem of Jesus' garment obtains healing to a chronically sick woman (Matt. 9:20).
A *little* oil and meal in reserve, when blessed by Elijah, multiplies and meets the needs of Elijah, the widow woman and her son for many months (1 Kings 17:12-14).
A *little* offering of two mites, given by a poor woman, is noticed by Jesus (Matt. 9:20).
A *little* possession, with the fear of the Lord, is better than great treasure and trouble (Prov. 15:16).
Though *little*, insects such as ants, rock badgers, locusts and spiders are exceedingly wise (Prov. 30:24).
Two *little* fish and five small loaves, blessed by Jesus, feeds more than 5,000 men (Matt. 6:38ff).
One who demonstrates a *little* faithfulness in small matters can be trusted with great matters (Matt. 25:21).

Negative *little* things:
A *little* backward glance turns Lot's wife into a pillar of salt (Gen. 19:26).
For the lack of a *little* oil, five of the ten virgins miss the Bridegroom's visitation (Luke 4:26-27).
A *little* lie spoken by Ananias and Sapphira cost them their lives (Acts 5:1-11).

Moses nearly loses his life over a *little* skin when his
wife refuses to circumcise their sons (Ex. 4:24-25).

A *little* sleep and a *little* slumber bring great poverty
(Prov. 6:10; 24:33).

A *little* negative conversation between the siblings,
Miriam and Aaron, costs time outside the camp
while she suffers leprosy (Num. 12:1-6).

A *little* favoritism shown by two parents, Rebekah and
Isaac, cause lifelong strife between the brothers,
Jacob and Esau (Gen. 27).

A *little* condoned immorality is like leaven, which leavens
the whole lump (1 Cor. 5:1-7).

A *little* fly in precious ointment ruins the ointment
(Eccles. 10:1).

The costly *little* thing in the life of the Shulamite woman
in chapter three is her unwillingness to leave the *little* pleasures of springtime for rocky cliffs of promise. In the Song's
fifth chapter she expresses her unwillingness to get her feet
dirty, as we will see in chapter five. Unwillingness to give up
little conveniences cost the Shulamite greatly.

At least four *little* and easily glossed-over things hinder
today's woman from seeking the Beloved with full abandon.
Women are often guilty of being control freaks, endless complainers, junk collectors, and *silly* competitors with other
women. Let's take a closer look at these little competitors of
communion with God.

**1. Ever since the eviction from the Garden of Eden
women struggle with an innate need to control or manipulate.** What are some of these little controlling tendencies? Feel
free to make your own additions to the list.

- Household finances
- Sex life
- Children
- Spouses
- Events
- Circumstances
- Boundaries
- In-laws

Examples:
- Eve easily is manipulated by the serpent and, in turn, encourages her husband to eat the forbidden fruit. Not once does she seek the counsel of her husband!
- Sarah manipulates Abram to take Hagar to bed to give her a child. The consequences of her attempt to help God out are seen in the Middle East today.
- Rebekah schemes to manipulate her husband to bless Jacob over Esau prematurely.
- Rachel, angry with her sister Leah over her own barrenness, devises a plan to obtain children through her handmaid.
- Leah manipulates the mandrake situation to her advantage to obtain another child (Gen. 30).
- Judah's daughter-in-law deceives him by masquerading as a prostitute in order to produce his child.
- Using sex, Delilah manipulates Samson to divulge his secrets.
- The Samaritan woman draws water at the well in the heat of the day to avoid painful rejection by others.

I hope you noticed how often I used the words *manipulate, deceive, devise,* and *schemes.* These all characterize a control freak!

On a more positive note, Mary, the mother of Jesus, demonstrates trust in God to bring to pass His promises. So great is her trust in God, she respectfully submits to Joseph's leadership in their move to Egypt and then back to Nazareth several years later. I find interesting the fact that after Mary's initial encounter with God, God guides their every move by speaking directly to Joseph. In her response to God's announcement to her Mary quotes 26 Old Testament passages; she has a high view of God and His power. Scripture indicates that after that first encounter God does not give further instructions to Mary about Jesus and their future. This is a radical truth for today's woman. Mary doesn't so much trust Joseph to do the right thing as she does trust God to lead Joseph. She has such a big view of God that she can trust Him to do that. Someone rightly said that faith is living without scheming.

God's basic plan for marriage is agreement (Amos 3:3) between a man and a woman who complement each other. When partners disagree, submission simply means that the wife trusts God to lead through her husband. She knows that God holds him, as the head of the home, ultimately accountable for the leadership of the family. Submission is meekness, not weakness. Biblical meekness is strength under control. The illustration of the harnessed ox exemplifies this. Meekness (or humility) is not weakness but rather controlled strength. **Unharnessed strength is beautiful but useless and destructive**; the harness that God places on lives serves only to make the wearer useful to God. Submission is the harness in marriage.

God uses the truth of submission to liberate me, not to imprison me. Stan is not threatened by my strength, because it is submitted to God. I am learning that submission is not the rejection of my personhood but the glad surrender of my life to God's ability, through my husband, to lead me. I don't lose anything in submission; submission allows me to acknowledge that I am a strong person instead of pretending I am not. This frees me to be the woman, wife, and mother that God intends me to be. The Shulamite loses nothing in the giving of herself completely to the Beloved.

The control freak can be cured. Jesus says,

> *"whoever desires to save his life will lose it, but whoever loses his life for my sake will find it"* (Matt. 16:25).

To surrender fully to the Sovereignty of God releases a woman from the need to control. What you believe about God will determine whether you practice submission in marriage, the workplace, finances, and pain and suffering. (More about that later!) Can He be trusted with the details of your life?

2. Women (and men) are born with a compulsion to complain. John Piper defines *self-pity* as inverted pride—the opposite of pride's boasting. Self-pity produces a complaining spirit. It is verbal pouting driven by a proud attitude of entitlement. It says, "God and others owe me something." Entitlement is a marked characteristic of the American culture.

We are altogether comfortable with accusing God of not being fair. Both genders are guilty of complaining. However the writer of Proverbs says the contentions of a wife are a continual dripping (Prov. 19:13) and that a very rainy day and a contentious woman are alike (Prov. 27:15). We women complain or become contentious when we:

- don't receive the attention we deserve;
- are not thanked or appreciated for what we have done;
- are not rewarded appropriately;
- are not properly recognized;

- have our time or resources taken advantage of;
- are overlooked for our contribution;
- perceive that our children, husband, or friends have
  not been treated fairly;
- feel left out or are not included.

Selfishly ambitious at heart, we demand that our needs be met immediately and appropriately; we cloak our wounded pride with tears, anger, and even prayer requests. We justify it with the words, "People aren't doing for me what I need for them to do for me."

Examples:
- Leah goes along with her father's deception of Jacob in marrying Jacob. She believes that her not marrying first, as the oldest and less attractive, is unfair.
- Hagar complains and actually runs away because of her unfair treatment by Sarai. God makes Hagar return and serve her mistress for 13 more years.
- Miriam is not satisfied to merely be Moses' sister but wants to be his spiritual peer (Num. 12).
- After leaving Israel, the children of Israel complain chronically when their needs are not met on demand (1 Cor. 10:10).

On a positive note, Hannah, instead of fighting with Peninnah, takes her complaint to the Lord (1 Sam. 1). Naomi, though bitter over the loss of her family, settles her complaints with God (Ruth 1:20-21). No woman is immune to life's hardships. Your reaction, however, is everything.

The cure for complaining is supplication in prayer and gratitude. *Be anxious for nothing but in everything, by prayer and supplication, with thanksgiving, let your requests be made known to God,*[26] says Paul. Cultivate an attitude of gratitude. No one owes me anything; anything I receive is more than I deserve. Stop and take a few minutes to read Psalm 37 and note the consequences and antidote for fretting or complaining.

3. Women are born with the need to collect things and stuff to feather the nest. Collections are as varied as are the women who collect. What are some of those collections?

- Figurines (angels, roosters, etc.,) and other dust collectors
- Beanie babies (Yep, I know grown women who collect them.)
- Clothing
- Shoes
- Jewelry pieces
- Conferences attended and studies completed
- Books
- Awards
- Music
- Antiques
- Elvis, Princess Diana, or other memorabilia
- Stamps

Jesus says that life doesn't consist of the abundance of things we possess. Collections make us feel significant. Collections define us. We think we are our degrees, our addresses, ring sizes, kid's achievements, and so forth. A. W. Tozer addressed this impulse to collect, "There is within the human heart a tough fibrous root of fallen life whose nature is to possess, always to possess."[27] Jesus refers to this tyranny of possessing when He says to His disciples,

> *"If any man will come after me, let him deny himself, and take up his cross, and follow me. For whosoever*

will save his life shall lose it: and whosoever will lose his life for my sake shall find it."

Examples:
- Lot's wife is unable to leave Sodom, because things are her life; things are more important than her family and obeying God.
- In order to embrace Christ, the rich young man must release things from first place in his heart and hands. Sadly, with hands full, he walks away from Jesus, who is Life (Matt. 19:20ff).
- Ananias and Sapphira lie to the Holy Spirit about selling their property and giving all of the proceeds to the ministry (Acts 5).

The only cure to collecting is stewardship or sacrifice. Jesus admonishes the collector to give as freely as he or she has received. I am reminded of an incident when our daughter was young and stingy. My father-in-law wisely advised me to teach her to give. Now she is generous to a fault! Only two things will endure forever: the souls of people and the Word of God. Invest well!

4. Women are born with a need to compete with other women. I once thought that men were more competitive than women were until I actively began to watch women as they compete with one another. Most competition among women is often subtle and silent; some is more obvious and ruthless. Some ways women compete:
- Prettiest nails
- Most fashionable
- Children's scholastic success
- Ministry opportunities

- Kids' physical/intellectual development
- Zip code or neighborhood
- Size of things (jewelry) and stuff (clothing)
- Education
- Career advancement
- Cars
- Social experiences
- Travels

Examples:
- Rachel and Leah compete for Jacob's favor by the number of children they produce (Genesis 29 and 30).
- Two women in the church at Philippi—Euodia and Syntyche—have some sort of quarrel going on which provokes a rebuke from Paul,

    "I implore Euodia and I implore Syntyche to be of the same mind in the Lord" (Phil. 4:2).

    I wonder what the dispute was over. When asked in heaven, "What was that all about?" I bet that at the Heavenly Ladies' Night Out they won't share the reason they were fussing. In the light of eternity much of what we fuss over now will appear absolutely trivial!
- Even the disciples get caught up in seeking personal greatness at the expense of others. Jesus said the greatest one is the servant of all. I have never seen a church competition on servanthood.

How do you slay a competitive spirit? By service to others. To His competitive disciples Jesus says,

"If anyone wants to be first, he must be the very last and the servant of all" (Mark 9:35).

I once heard Henry Blackaby put a great spin on servanthood. In his message he said, "Christians don't have a problem with service as long as they aren't treated like servants." Jesus washes the disciple's feet and expects us to follow His example. Paul urges believers to

"let nothing be done through selfish ambition or conceit but in lowliness of mind let each esteem others better than himself" (Phil. 2:3).

Competing with the one whose feet we are washing is utterly impossible; ministering to someone with whom we are in competition or to be ministered to by someone with whom we are in competition also is impossible. The Shulamite doesn't compete with the daughters of Jerusalem. She discovers contentment and significance in her relationship with the Beloved.

Other little foxes that spoil the vine: unbelief and hardness of heart.

In our lack of wisdom we sometimes consider unbelief as a *little* thing. Jesus addresses unbelief and defines it as *"hardness of heart."* His teaching clearly illustrates that this is a timeless problem and that it requires timely remedies.

Hardness of heart can be wrapped up in the deceptive packaging of spirituality and sometimes is difficult to detect. Often those who follow most closely to Jesus have the greatest difficulty with complaining, controlling, competing, and collecting, which all are a result of unbelief. (Americans are the most liberated peoples in the world and yet are the most demanding.) Jesus confronts the disciples about their hardness of heart in their response to His approaching them in the middle of the lake during a storm (Mark 6:45-52; 8:13-17) and rebukes them during a post-resurrection appearance (16:14).

What exactly is *hardness of heart*? The Greek word *poroo* is a small piece of stone broken off from a larger one. The verb means *to harden, make hard like a stone*, or *callous and insensible to the touch*. One scholar defines it as "a loss of feeling" or an "inability to feel." In the New Testament it applies only in a spiritual sense to the hearts or minds of people.[28]

Notice the opposite: *porous*—permeable to fluids, permeable to outside influences, capable of being penetrated.[29] The hardened heart does not receive the Word of God but repels both its messenger and its message. Compare a sponge to a stone. The sponge absorbs the water and the rock repels the water; the Word of God runs off the hard heart.

Little stones cause more stumbling than do big rocks. Because of its tiny size the very thing that will cause a person to stumble is easy to overlook. Are you allowing a *little* thing to remain in your life? Left unresolved such things create hardness of heart and, like the fox, do much mischief. How many little foxes can spoil the Christian life! To name a few:

- pride, an unwillingness to humble oneself (Prov. 6:19)
- little compromises (receiving too much change at grocery store and not being honest about it; using expired coupons hoping they won't be noticed) (Rom. 12:17)
- giving or listening to negative reports about others (Lev. 19:16)
- transfer of love from husband to children (Titus 2:4)

- use of idle words or inappropriate language
    (Mt. 19:36; Col. 3:8)
- a married person's flirting with a person of the opposite
    gender (Prov. 7:14-20)
- griping and complaining (Phil. 2:13)
- living unfulfilled dreams through the children
    (Mt. 11:1-13)
- unwillingness to forgive an offense (Mark 11:25)
- being easily angered (Eph. 4:26)
- not meeting the needs of my spouse (1 Cor. 7:3)
- keeping a messy house (Titus 2:5)
- partiality to the rich or to the poor (Lev. 19:15)
- bearing a grudge against others (Lev. 19:18)
- love for the things of the world (1 John 2:15-17;
    Jas. 4:4)
- living for the approval of others (Luke 16:15; John 5:44)

What are the *little* things that spoil your vine? Are they complaining, controlling, competing, or collecting? Take a penny and hold it in front of your right eye while you close your left one. What does the penny block from your view? Great things are obstructed by these seemingly insignificant little pennies. The closer to the eye the coin is held, the less one sees in the distance; the house across the street disappears as does the sunset. A tiny coin held close to the eye obstructs objects many times larger than the coin itself.

One Sunday after church, while I ate at a cafeteria-style restaurant, I noticed a server intently watching a table across from ours. Sitting at the table were a grandmother, a grown child and spouse, and three grandchildren. Every time the child in the high chair dropped food on the floor, the grand-mother kicked it further under the table. The waitress shook her head in disgust. Then I noticed why. The grandmother had a nametag on her lapel which proclaimed her name and title (pianist of so-and-so church). Testimony lost. A *little* fox—food kicked under the table—stole her Christian witness to the server. The *little* things steal so much.

Love's intermission (2:16-17)

The Shulamite:
"My lover is mine and I am his.
He browses among the lilies."

(To her beloved):
"Until the day breaks
And the shadows flee,
Turn, my lover,
And be like a gazelle
Or like a young stag
On the rugged hills."

So far in the Song we have reveled in the lovers' mutual affirmation, we have admired the Shulamite's testimony to the daughters of Jerusalem of the Beloved's attributes, and we have followed the Beloved's invitation to intimacy. Time now for an intermission. This intermission allows the lovers to fulfill normal activities of life. Throughout the Song the man and woman experience togetherness and separation, work and play. Intimacy unpunctuated by labor leads to self-absorption and a pharisaic form of pride. Jesus never says that working or toiling is wrong, but toil apart from intimacy is burdensome. Jesus condemns the Pharisees for neglecting good deeds while presenting themselves as righteous. Their religious activity is an excuse to ignore the needs of others (Matt 23:14, 23).

Leading a balanced life between the awareness of constant love and the demands and responsibilities required indicates a maturation of love. The purpose of the honeymoon is to explore righteously the intimacy of love's sexual expression without any distractions. Once the honeymoon is over, challenges immediately arise. They create an atmosphere for the blending together of differing personalities and responsibilities. The Christian life is no different. It is a life of devotion and duty.

The Shulamite states what is obvious but often forgotten. Whether involved with the Beloved or separated because of vineyard duties, the reality of their relationship does not change. While they tend the vineyard or feed the flock, love still is active. Don't make times of physical separation to be times of feeling insecure or guilty but times of joy and anticipation of the next encounter. I am no less Jesus' when I am out shopping for groceries, answering the phone at work, or attending an art exhibit with my children. I am no more His when I am in my recliner having morning devotions. I am no less married while I am at work and no more married while I am at home. The Beloved is no less hers while he feeds his flock than when he is at home by her side in the palace.

As the day runs its course and the shadows of evening are in decline, darkness makes its approach. As a good shepherd the Beloved has spent the day among the lilies feeding the flocks. The Shulamite urges him to return quickly. He is eager to be reunited with the Shulamite. Duty is an expression of trust—the doing well in absence as in presence.

Private devotion and public service

In his letters to the Corinthian believers during his absence from them Paul demonstrates this attitude (2 Cor. 10:11). Paul has the same expectations for the Philippian believers whether he is present or absent (Phil 1:27). Paul rejoices in the Colossians' steadfastness in both his presence and absence. His presence or absence make no difference (Col. 2:5). He admonishes the believers in whatever they do in word and deed to do all in the name of the Lord Jesus (Col. 3:17). He then urges wives to submit to their husbands as fitting in the Lord, husbands to love their wives, children to obey their parents, and bondservants to obey their masters. In verses 23 and 24 he then summarizes all their duties:

And whatever you do, do it heartily, as to the Lord and not to men, knowing that from the Lord you will receive the reward of the inheritance; for you serve the Lord Christ.

He makes no distinction between work and worship, duty and delight. Working well is worship!

Before God and *in the presence of God* are phrases Paul repeatedly uses to describe everything he does. This phrase, *enopion*, means *in the presence of and as marking the manner, and especially the sincerity with which anything is done before God or in the sight of God, meaning God is present and witness.*[30]

Paul lives in the presence of God; his God-awareness leads him to

renounce the hidden things of shame, not walking in craftiness nor handling the word of God deceitfully, but by manifestation of the truth commending ourselves to every man's conscience in the sight of God (2 Cor. 4:2).

Paul concludes his call to apostleship with

*Now concerning the things which I write to you,
indeed, before God, I do not lie* (Gal. 1:20).

Continually he lived aware of the presence of God. We
would do well to live our lives in His presence in both work
and worship. Hudson Taylor, missionary to China during the
early 1900's, sums it up perfectly,

The intense activity of our times may lead to zeal in
service to the neglect of personal communion, but such
neglect will not only lesson the value of the service,
but tend to incapacitate us for the highest service.[31]

Devotion is what makes duty profitable.

Chapter 3

Love's Troubled Waters

In the previous chapter we rejoice together with the Shulamite as we eavesdrop on her conversation with the daughters of Jerusalem. She regales them with tales of the Beloved's banner, banquet house, protection, and invitation. The Shulamite experiences total pleasure and satisfaction as she and the Beloved spend intimate time together. We are there when she receives his invitation to go with him—to leave the glories of spring for the rustic, solitary cleft of the rock. His invitation to the rocky clefts remains unanswered. The Shulamite has been warned of the little thieves of intimacy and admonished to capture the little foxes before damage is done. As we join the Shulamite in her search in the city (instead of in the clefts of the rock where he promised he would be found) where she finds her Beloved, we take delight in the Shulamite's new discoveries regarding the Beloved and their relationship.

When our first child, Jennifer, was several months old, she often woke in the night (as most babies do). My husband told me she would learn to go back to sleep if I didn't run in to check on her. He made me stay in bed (he actually held me down) while she cried herself back to sleep. The first several nights were horrible. Not only was I distressed at her crying, I also was angry at Stan's seeming coldness toward her tears. After a week the crying (both mine and hers) diminished to a whimper. In two weeks she began sleeping through the entire night. Though painful to implement at first, this method was so successful that I did the same when my boys were born. Early on in her relationship with the Beloved the Shulamite is just as juvenile—only she is not a baby but a woman. As she wakes in the night, she cries out for him, but he is not there. Like a good parent the Beloved briefly resists her cries—not because he is unloving and difficult, but because she has a few things she needs to learn about herself and about her Beloved.

Intimacy's departure (3:1)

Throughout the Song the lovers experience periods of distance and closeness—such is the reality of love. The Shulamite has, in the past, joyfully experienced intimacy to a certain degree. The third chapter opens with the Shulamite in a lonely bed; she struggles to locate her absent lover. The Song's author introduces us to the couple's first season of trouble. (In chapter five we will look at a second season of trouble).

> "*By night on my bed I sought the one I love;*
> *I sought him, but I did not find him.*"

An empty bed

The empty bed testifies to a missing delight—a missing treasure. Her mood changes progressively from yearning for his presence to fear of loss and abandonment to panicky action. She lies in her bed, half asleep, half awake, and restlessly yearns for her Beloved's presence beside her. The darkness, not the light, highlights his absence. He is not where he should be at a time when she needs him. This makes his physical absence intolerable. Her wild thoughts and her utter distress drive her to desperation—hence, a panic attack.

Anxiety is a treasure-revealer. Jesus speaks of the heart's treasure,

> *"For where your treasure is, there your heart will be also."*

Anxiety is a treasure-revealer. When a person's true treasure is disturbed, that person will react with the fury of a hornet's nest hit by a stone. Not only do we get upset when someone meddles with our treasures, we also spend considerable time thinking about our heart's attachments. An observer easily sees our treasure by identifying the subject that laces our conversations and captures much of our attention.

When what we delight in goes missing, no obstacle is too large to hinder our recovery of that delight. This is true of the Shulamite; room to room she searches without result. He is gone. The anxiety over her lost treasure drives her from the comforts of home into the night and the dangers lurking in dark streets. Isaiah speaks of the temptation to light our own fire when the darkness is present:

> *Who among you fears the Lord?*
> *Who obeys the voice of His Servant?*
> *Who walks in darkness*
> *And has no light?*
> *Let him trust in the name of the Lord*
> *And rely upon his God.*
> *Look, all you who kindle a fire,*
> *Who encircle yourselves with sparks:*
> *Walk in the light of your fire and in the sparks*
> *   you have kindled*
> *This you shall have from My hand:*
> *You shall lie down in torment* (Isa. 50:10-11).

The prophet laments for those who kindle their own fire. Many women wake up to an empty bed (both physically and emotionally); they simply replace the emptiness with something else. Passion and intimacy must be carefully guarded; once romance is absent, the enemy offers many tempting substitutes or "ghost lovers" (things that make us feel good or special), such as romantic novels, erotic movies, comfort food, shopping or excessive spending, coping medications, overemphasis on the outward, and adulterous relationships.

The list is endless. Our appetites reveal our hunger and what we feed on reveals our values. Amy Carmichael quotes Ralph Waldo Emerson as saying, "Beware of all you set your heart upon—for it shall surely be yours." Both what we pursue and what we don't pursue reveal what we love and therefore what we prioritize. If our priorities shape our habits, then our habits reveal our priorities.

Everyone pursues something. Everyone invests in what he or she perceives as treasures (hobbies, relationships, ministry, cars and houses, retirement plans, grandchildren, career, etc.). In his book *Finding God*, Larry Crabb describes this pursuit as an attempt to make life outside the Garden of Eden a little more as we imagine it should be:

> All our troublesome passions spring from this core passion to make our present lives better: distorted appetites for food or sex, bizarre urges that overwhelm us at the least convenient time, consuming desires to like ourselves better, a frantic determination to succeed personally or professionally, an insistence that spiritual victory translate into a comfortable life that no tragedy or tension can disrupt, a lust for revenge against those who have hurt us. We are passionately determined to make our lives less painful, and we will do whatever it

takes to reach this goal in a disappointing, sometimes pleasurable, and maddeningly uncertain world.[32]

Furthermore, Crabb defines the pursuit by how they:

• Find some way to make their present lives happier;
• Influence the people and material of their world to cooperate with them in their pursuit.[33]

Truly, their greatest treasure is the fulfillment of their own desires.

On the other hand, if our treasure in this life is to know God, then:

• The empty bed testifies that life has more to it than personal comfort.
• Remaining in bed leads only to depression and despondency.
• The empty bed cannot be filled with other occupants such as church activity and "doing things for the Lord." Spiritual substitutes cannot replace the relationship with the Beloved.

George Burrows determines that these absences "test the strength of our faith and steadfastness of our love; they lead to deeper searching for secret sins; they advance humility by making us feel our weakness and our dependence on God."[34] The writer Rutherford describes these absences:

As nights and shadows are good for flowers, and moonlight and dews are better than a continual sun, so is Christ's absence of special use, and it hath some nourishing virtue in it, and giveth sap to humility, and putteth an edge on hunger, and furnisheth a fair field to faith to put forth itself.[35]

Burrows also records John Owen's similar acknowledgment of this truth:

The Lord Jesus Christ is pleased sometimes to withdraw himself from the spiritual experience of believers, as unto any refreshing sense of his love, or the fresh communications of consolatory graces. Those who never had experiences of any such thing, who never had any refreshing communion with him, cannot be sensible of his absence; they never were so of his presence. But those whom he hath visited, to whom he hath given his loves, with whom he hath made his abode, whom he hath refreshed, relieved, and comforted, in whom he hath lived in the power of his grace, they know what it is to be forsaken by him, though but for a moment.[36]

The Beloved's absence enlarges the Shulamite's heart. It makes her capable of giving and receiving even more love. Likewise these absences (and we experience many in the Christian life) are the Beloved's opportunity for us to identify and remove other occupants from our beds of love and enlarge our capacity and hunger to know Him. Do you have any rivals for His affection in your heart? Ask Him now to identify and help you remove the substitutes, the "other" occupants, from your bed.

Truly "absence does make the heart grow fonder." God ordains periods of absence to purify our desires and teach us to walk by faith and not by sight. Absences—unavoidable and necessary—are profitable for our spiritual good and growth.

The writer of Hebrews tells us that the only thing that we can do that pleases God is to trust Him— to have faith in Him (Heb. 11:6). Every believer has to discover what the Shulamite learns: absences are a part of life for God's children. At first we feel sorry for ourselves and question His love. As we push through our discomfort, trust His unfailing love, and begin to walk by faith, He may very well restore the sense of His presence again.

The benefits of such absences:

- They signal new opportunities to walk by faith, as we lean on the last light God has given.
- They show confidence from God that He trusts the new believer's growth in grace.
- They shore up the new believer's faith by taking faith from the arena of feelings (the "seen" things) to simple trust (the "unseen" things). See 2 Corinthians 4:16-18.

Someone once said that you either are entering, are in the middle of, or are recovering from some sort of spiritual discomfort. Know that a season of absence is for your good and your growth. It is the stuff of which sanctification is made. He loves you and will find you when you arrive at the end of yourself. Meanwhile don't fill the empty bed with substitutes or quit because the search seems futile or becomes difficult.

What do you do when He seems absent or His presence does not seem real to you? Duty and devotion demand that we persevere in our pursuit of Him. In my life the following activities have been beneficial during these necessary but disturbing times:

- Pray and tell the Beloved how you feel. He wants to hear your voice and to see your face.
- Meditate on Scripture. During these times the Psalms have always comforted me. Take a few moments to read aloud Psalms 42 and 43.
- Confess and turn from substitute occupants.
- Grieve over His absence. Grief over loss is natural and needed.
- Get out of bed!
- Long for Him by listening to praise songs.
- Don't neglect spending time with other believers.
- Read good books. The bibliography at the end of this book lists books that have been a source of encouragement during my own periods of absence and search.
- Don't waste precious time watching daytime TV and videos. They only prolong the season!
- Perhaps you can share with a mature believer your difficulty. Being accountable in difficult times helps you defeat the deadening tendency to attract other occupants (other people, destructive habits, depression, etc.) to your spiritual bed.

The poem, *The Weaver*, is wonderfully encouraging.

The Weaver

My life is but a weaving
Between the Lord and me,
I cannot choose the colors
He worketh steadily.

Ofttimes He weaveth sorrow,
And I in foolish pride
Forget He sees the upper
And I, the underside.

Not till the loom is silent
And the shuttles cease to fly
Shall God unroll the canvas
And explain the reason why.

The dark threads are as needful
In the Weaver's skillful hand
As the threads of gold and silver
In the pattern He has planned.[37]

Intimacy's restoration (3:2-6)

In the previous section we note the Shulamite's acute awareness of her Beloved's absence. Let's observe her reaction to his absence. Though the Beloved controls the length of absence, the Shulamite determines the urgency of the search. Driven by desire, with no regard for the possible dangers of the night, she leaves her house and searches the streets. It is an irrational and impractical search.

"I will rise now," I said,
"And go about the city;
In the streets and in the squares
I will seek the one I love."
I sought him, but I did not find him.
The watchmen who go about the city found me;
I said, "Have you seen the one I love?"

I will arise. Recall the invitation in 2:10, 13 to go away with him? In the light of the day, going away with him would have been easier. Instead, she went to bed! Darkness easily can justify her delaying the search until morning. She does, however, the urgent thing: she gets out of bed.

I will arise now, in the night. The search is by night. The NIV translates this *as all night long*; the NEB translates this as *night after night.* No quick search will do; this longing awakens an arduous search that continues until he is found.

I will search the streets. Her cry is the language of a soul in anguish. Where is he? To no avail she searches the streets and the square. Her love, not regulated by his voice and leading but rather moved by her own sense of loss and discomfort, brings her into circumstances which are quite unsuitable to the Shulamite. She is alone in the dark as she launches her search. The watchmen of the city find her; they are useless and are unable to reunite her with her Beloved.

I sought him, but I did not find him. Sought, a common Old Testament verb, is used both literally and figuratively. It is always a conscious act and frequently requires a great deal of effort with no guarantee of success.[38] In verses 1-2 three times she mentions her fruitless search. This is no casual hunt; she is desperate to be reunited with her Beloved.

Her lack of response to the earlier invitation (2:10-13) manifests an air of indifference or reluctance. She wants to experience him where doing so is comfortable for her. His absence moves her beyond selfish indifference to deliberate pursuit.

Perhaps that explains the futile seeking of the Lord that is the experience of so many; they either want God on their terms, or they are indifferent to His absence.

How can she who has been so intelligent as to say, "*He feeds his flocks among the lilies*" (2:16), now make such a mistake as to seek him at night in such dangerous surroundings? Her search is hopeless as she looks for him in the wrong place. Such is the consequence of neglecting the voice of the Beloved and his invitation to the cleft's heights. The cleft in the rocks, which seems to be the most dangerous place, is instead, the safest place of all; because there, he promises to commune with her.

For the believer, these verses illustrate the earnestness of the soul in seeking Jesus in the time of His absence. During these times when we feel alone and deserted, we learn to walk by faith rather than by sight. **Test faith, because only through conflict can you turn it into personal possession.** How does a woman know when she possesses genuine faith? Only through the testing of trials.

His absence deepens desire; his discovery heightens appreciation, authenticates faith, and revisits past delights. By faith we find that He has been there with us all along; the keen awareness of His presence is missing. Grace is His meeting us where (in the empty streets) we seek Him.

These verses also challenge the believer to consider where Jesus can be found; Hebrews 13:13 describes one such place as outside the camp, the place of reproach. When life is easy, with circumstances sweet, our spiritual senses become dull and dormant. Nothing like difficulty to awaken desire! Only as Cleopas and his companion leave Jerusalem after the Passion Week do they encounter Jesus. Their hopes have been dashed, their Redeemer crucified; they have no point remaining in Jerusalem, so they leave (Luke 24:13-27). Scarcely have they left the city (seven miles out) when Jesus appears and walks with them, breaks bread with them, and opens their eyes to the reality of His presence.

"Scarcely had I passed by them,
When I found the one I love.
I held him and would not let him go,
Until I had brought him to the house of my mother,
And into the chamber of her who conceived me."

The search is over. The drama ends as suddenly as it has begun. The Beloved does not cast her off or even chide her for not answering his invitation or for looking for him in all the wrong places. At such times many women make the mistake of despairing and reproaching themselves; instead, they can rejoice when they are found. Both the period of absence and the search are necessary elements of a growing relationship. Welcome to the Christian life! I like the quote often attributed to G. K. Chesterton, "The problem with Christianity is not that is has been tried and found wanting but that it has been found difficult and untried." When she finds him, the Shulamite holds him and does not let him go. She brings him to the house of her mother. Burrows describes the oriental houses of her day:

> Their chambers are large and spacious, one of them frequently serving a whole family. At one end of each chamber there is a little gallery raised four or five feet, with a balustrade and doubtless a veil to draw in the front of it. Here they place their beds . . . Seeking thus to enjoy confidential fellowship . . . where there may be no intrusion . . . expressing the anxiety to guard against anything likely to make him withdraw.[39]

In the first chapter the Beloved brings the Shulamite into his house and into his private chambers; he withholds nothing from her. Now she brings him to the home of her mother. You are often amazed at what you learn about someone when you see them in an environment in which they are most comfortable. The return to the home of her mother is a rite of passage for the Shulamite. It reveals a new level of personal comfort with their relationship as it is exposed to the knowing eyes of her mother.

The restoration of this relationship brings relief from the agony experienced by the loss and the search. Such relief compels the Shulamite to protect this tender and restored love:

"I charge you, O daughters of Jerusalem,
By the gazelles or by the does of the field,
Do not stir up nor awaken love
Until it pleases."

Love is as sensitive as the gazelles and the does of the fields, which run away at the slightest provocation. Again in the Song the Shulamite charges the daughters of Jerusalem not to intrude on this newly restored relationship. Protect certain times and seasons in our lives and shelter them from the curiosity of others.

The search is as vital to the Christian life as are the results of the search. God's goal is not our personal comfort or happiness. He desires that we pursue Him with all our hearts. The valuable lessons learned while at a distance from the Lord may serve as a dark cloud—the backdrop for the rainbow of God's marvelous promises and grace.

We are satisfied with so little. To intensify and purify our desires God sometimes allows what we have to be removed. Sometimes, as our infant daughter had to learn, crying doesn't earn immediate gratification. In fact immediate gratification is more harmful than it is good. The search both reveals and builds character. The Christian life is a process, not an end. Second Peter 1:5-8 gives a list of characteristics (virtue, knowledge, self-control, perseverance, godliness, brotherly kindness, and love); add these to your faith. God designs specific trials for the addition of these very characteristics.

The Shulamite finds that a love relationship is more than just receiving acceptance and love from the Beloved. Trials challenge her to maturity; they cause her to pursue or develop personal characteristics that, in turn, enlarge her capacity to more fully appreciate his love. Many marriages fail because partners fail during seasons of crisis and pursue their own desires and agenda over the needs their spouses.

Intimacy's transformation (3:6)

Absence is the father and *search* is the mother, who together give birth to new insight. New discoveries are made that otherwise would have been left unearthed. His absence and her search make possible the revelation of things which before were hidden. Unusual treasures emerge from the wilderness.

"Who is this coming out of the wilderness
Like pillars of smoke,
Perfumed with myrrh and frankincense,
With all the merchant's fragrant powders?"

Though some versions credit the Shulamite as the one asking this question, most commentators indicate that this question is directed to the Shulamite by another. One of the daughters of Jerusalem or a family member or the author of the poem may be interjecting himself or herself into the poem. "Whoever it may be, it is certain that the question is not a request for information. It is a rhetorical question whose answer is obvious."[40] "Wow! Look who's coming out of the wilderness!" It is an announcement and an exclamation of admiration. As the wilderness yields its fruit, three things become immediately clear.

One, she exits the wilderness. The phrase "is meant to evoke an atmosphere of awe, majesty, almost of unreality . . . appearing mysteriously and without explanation. The perfumes and powders of the ancient apothecary are compounded from plants growing in the wilderness. It is only here, in wilderness experiences, that we are able to develop the graces of Christian character that are so pleasing and refreshing to others."[41] The most bitter women I have known are those who are hardened rather than softened in the wilderness.

Second, her appearance is changed as a result of her wilderness experience. The fact that her appearance is described as *pillars of clouds* is not surprising. God promises the children of Israel, as they approach the wilderness, that He will be to them a pillar of cloud by day and a pillar of fire by night (Ex. 13:17-22). Charles Swindoll comments on Moses' 40 years on the backside of the desert:

> The desert is where God speaks, where He communi-
> cates some of His most important messages to us.
> Apart from the desert experience, you and I might live
> out our lives without ever hearing or knowing what the
> God of the universe desires to tell us. The wilderness-
> like desert changes that. In that lonely place, you find
> yourself stripped of all the things you hang on to for
> comfort—all the stuff you felt you needed through life
> but really didn't need at all.[42]

Though painful, the wilderness experience changes her for the better. Her capacity to know and experience the Beloved has been enlarged. As a result, she glows!

Finally, for her to go through this experience alone is necessary. Where were these friends, these daughters of Jerusalem, when the Beloved finds her alone? Isolation is always a part of the desert experience. Had they joined the search, they only would have been bystanders—observers. The Shulamite appears out of the wilderness alone and is all the better for it. Someone has said, "God doesn't mass-produce His saints. He hand-tools each one, and it always takes longer than we expect."

The Bible is replete with stories about God's heroes who pass through difficult times and experience the distance and recovery of God's presence. As he tells the story of Jesus' baptism and subsequent temptation encounter, Matthew recounts the most familiar wilderness experience:

Then Jesus was led up by the Spirit into the wilderness to be tempted by the devil. And when He had fasted forty days and forty nights, afterward He was hungry. Now when the tempter came to Him, he said, "If You are the Son of God, command that these stones become bread." But He answered and said, "It is written, 'Man shall not live by bread alone, but by every word that proceeds from the mouth of God.'" Then the devil took Him up into the holy city, set Him on the pinnacle of the temple, and said to Him, "If You are the Son of God, throw Yourself down. For it is written: 'He shall give His angels charge over you,' and, 'In their hands they shall bear you up, Lest you dash your foot against a stone.'" Jesus said to him, "It is written again, 'You shall not tempt the Lord your God.'" Again, the devil took Him up on an exceedingly high mountain, and showed Him all the kingdoms of the world and their glory. And he said to Him, "All these things I will give

*You if You will fall down and worship me." Then Jesus
said to him, "Away with you, Satan! For it is written,
'You shall worship the Lord your God, and Him only
you shall serve.'" Then the devil left Him, and behold,
angels came and ministered to Him.*[43]

During the tests that Satan throws at Him, Jesus remains
totally human. That is why He identifies with us in our problems. His temptations cover three areas:

- **His appetite (verses 2-4)** He has genuine needs; He
  is hungry. Satan challenges Him to feed Himself
  instead of waiting on God for His provision. Many,
  failing to wait on God's provision, go into debt or
  gamble. Hoping for the big payout, they meet their
  needs their own way—many times to their detriment.
- **His authority (verses 5-7)** He can get what He needs
  by manipulating the natural laws established at creation. The devil calls on Him to throw Himself
  down to force God into proving that He is His
  Father and that He will protect Him. God does not
  need to prove Himself to any person.
- **His ambition (verses 8-10)** The kingdoms of the
  world can be His without the cross, but the price is
  worship—worship of the rebellious angel, Satan.
  Ambition invites us to exchange the eternal for the
  temporal; this exchange entices but eventually
  impoverishes.

This wilderness experience prepares him for an even bigger test: the Cross.

The 40 years on the backside of the desert are educational for Moses. Though he does not realize it, once the children of Israel are released from Egypt, he will spend another 40 years in the desert.

How does the Shulamite benefit from this brief wilderness experience?
- She refines her values/needs—she is made aware of an empty bed.
- She refocuses her goals—she can't live without his presence. *"I will arise."*
- She revives worship—she identifies her treasure, *"Have you seen the one I love?"*
- She realizes meaning/worth—her return from that experience changes her for the better.
- She recognizes the enemy—the watchmen don't have a clue how to help her find the Beloved.
- She revisits his promise—the search won't be futile, for he has said, *"Rise up and come away."*

We can easily become comfortable with our spiritual lives and in doing so develop a demanding spirit—a demand that we immediately have relief! We conquer a demanding spirit when we learn that we may not get what we want when we want it. When this truth burns home, we realize that God is not our servant; we are His. No one is immune to difficulties. **Difficulties reveal character.** Paul tells the believer to endure hardship as a good soldier. Solomon reminds the believer, *If you faint in the day of adversity, your strength is small* (Prov. 24:10).

Ignoring the cries of my babies until they learned to sleep through the night sounds heartless. The action, though painful, achieved the desired result—my kids learned that self-centered crying doesn't get them a thing! It nipped in the bud a demanding spirit. Sometimes you, too, as you cry like an infant, will long for God to show you pity. You may rail at Him for not answering your prayer immediately. You may fume and even threaten Him that you will quit this Christian life if He doesn't act at your bidding. Hold on! He will wait patiently through your tantrum until you, too, realize that you have nowhere else to go for true joy.

Intimacy's discovery (3:7-11)

Once intimacy is restored, the Shulamite experiences and appreciates the Beloved's kingly splendor. He is so much more than she first anticipated; the implications of being in relationship with him are far greater than she previously thought. Before the absence, search, and recovery the Shulamite has a limited view of the Beloved. Before, she sees him as a prince, a shepherd, the one who feeds his flocks among the lilies. As a result of the wilderness experience the relationship matures as she rises to the challenge of relating to the Beloved as a King. Notice the majesty of the King's entourage and carriage:

Behold, it is Solomon's couch,
With sixty valiant men around it,
Of the valiant of Israel.
They all hold swords,
Being expert in war.
Every man has his sword on his thigh
Because of fear in the night.

His caravan
The caravan, obviously a royal procession bearing the king, is accompanied by 60 valiant men who protect the mag-

nificent caravan. *Valiant* is from the Hebrew word translated *warrior, the heroes or champions among the armed forces.*[44] They are not novices but battle-hardened veterans—the elite of all troops. The importance of this entourage is compared with the valiant men who guard King David; in 2 Samuel 23:8-39 the Bible records the elite forces guarding David. David has 37 mighty men compared to the Beloved's 60. David's top three are noted for their tremendous valor.

- Adino kills 800 men at one time.
- Eleazar fights so veraciously that his sword actually sticks to his hand.
- Shammah takes out an entire troop at one time.

Not only are these noble fighting men, they are fiercely loyal. Thirsty, David mentions how good a drink of water from the well in Bethlehem (encamped by the Philistine army) would taste. What do his chief three do but go fetch him a cup!

- Abishai is another of David's heroic fighters. He takes down 300 fighting men at one time.
- Benaiah is a second-generation valiant man, the son of a valiant man. He kills two lionlike heroes of Moab (a lion in the midst of a pit on a snowy day and a spectacular Egyptian warrior.)

Solomon's 60 men of similar heroic material are nearly twice in number as David's valiant men.

The cargo of the caravan is precious; the king takes no chances with the safety of his bride. Foremost on the Beloved's mind is protection of the Shulamite. Should bandits appear at night and terrorize the bride, the soldiers are ready for them.[45] The Bible tells us that Jesus our King, who slays his enemies with a sword from His mouth, still travels with *ten thousands of His saints* and is called *the Lord of hosts* (armies).

The ability of our Beloved to protect us is seen in the following verses:

- He is able to keep me from stumbling (Jude 24).
- He is able to present me faultless before God (Jude 25).
- He is able to deliver me from danger (Dan. 4:17).
- He is able to perform all of His promises (Rom. 4:20-21).
- He is able to make me stand (Rom. 14:4).
- He is able to do exceedingly, abundantly above all I ask or think (Eph. 3:20-21).
- He is able to subdue all things unto Himself (Phil. 3:20-21).
- He is able to aid those who are tempted (Heb. 2:18).
- He is able to keep that which is committed to Him (2 Tim. 1:12).
- He is able to save to the uttermost those who come to God through Him (Heb. 7:25).

Though unseen the army of the Lord surrounds his people; God sends them to surround and protect us from evil. The Word of God is a sword, which the writer of Hebrews describes as living and powerful (Heb. 4:12). It equips for every good work. Other protecting devices are:

- An active prayer life (Eph. 6:18)
- The counsel of godly people (Prov. 24:6)

- The spoken testimony (Rev. 12:11)
- The active avoidance of evil (Eph. 4:25-27)
- The power of submission (Eph. 5:21). This submission means that we trust God to work through those authorities He places in our lives.

Why is the caravan so heavily guarded? Because of fear in the night. In antiquity, because of the Arabs' audacity, weddings often turned into mourning by enemies lying in ambush:

> They went up and hid themselves under the cover of the mountains; where they lifted up their eyes and looked, and behold there was much ado and great carriage; and the bridegroom came forth and his friends and brethren to meet them, with drums and instruments of music and many weapons. Then Jonathan and those that were with him rose up against them from the place where they lay in ambush, and made a slaughter of them in such sort as many fell down dead, and the remnant fled into the mountains; and they took all their spoils. Thus was the marriage turned into mourning and the noise of their melody into lamentation.[46]

Fear is a very real emotion. The spirit of this age is fear (2 Tim 1:7). At the end of the 20th century Y2K drove individuals, companies, and countries to spend millions of dollars many believed was unnecessary. Fear dominates our world today—the fear of global warming, fear of terrorism, fear of conservative Christianity, and so on. Because fears abound (some real/some perceived), protection is needed.

The peace of God waits to stand guard over the hearts of those who pray about everything and worry about nothing. Women must rely on the weapons the Beloved provides and trust in His weapons for protection (her husband, pastor, fellow believers, and a life saturated by the Word and prayer) as we journey on this pilgrimage called the Christian life. We have insurance for our cars, homes, and physical health, but few people really take the time to insure their spiritual health. Surely the Shulamite's confidence is bolstered as she experiences the protection found in the traveling escort of the caravan; so our faith is bolstered by the companions of the Christian life—prayer, the Word of God, and the interaction with others who are like-minded.

The carriage

Notice the material constructing the carriage (3:9-10):

Of the wood of Lebanon
Solomon the King made himself a palanquin:
He made its pillars of silver,
Its support of gold,
Its seat of purple,
Its interior paved with love by the daughters of
Jerusalem.

No wonder thieves are such a threat! Not only is the carriage valued for its occupants but also for the priceless materials used for its construction (like the difference between a moped and a Lexus)!

Though commentators disagree on whether this carriage is stationary or portable, the majority assert that it is portable. "The *palanquin* means a kind of sedan chair or open vehicle, in which persons in the East are carried on men's shoulders."[47] Riding in a palanquin is an exciting and humbling experience.

In order to see Myanmar's famous Golden Rock, a palanquin carries visitors up the side of the mountain. As I recently visited this historic site, four scrawny young men hoisted me onto their shoulders in a simple palanquin, a seat tied to two large bamboo poles. Their shoulders poured sweat as they carried me for several miles up the side of the mountain. On their red and sweaty backs I arrived well-rested and sweatless. I was humbled by their labor on my behalf. Sitting high on their shoulders, I was able to relax and enjoy my surroundings without the distractions that accompany walking.

The materials used to construct the Shulamite's palanquin certainly are more regal than were those that used to make the one on which I rode. No bamboo poles are these. They are cedar from Lebanon, and are covered ornately with precious gold and silver. The litter or seat is large enough for several occupants. While we cannot be sure of the actual design of the carriage, we can be sure this carriage is like none other, for it is designed by the King himself. Such a carriage requires a closer inspection. Take a look.

The wood of Lebanon represents *fragrance and incorruptibility*. His carriage is made of the very best wood—wood from Lebanon. This wood is imported by King Solomon for the building of the temple for the name of the Lord God of Israel (1 Kings 5:5-9). After the 70 years of exile in Babylon, Zerubbabel leads Israel in its "second exodus" back to the Promised Land. He purchases cedar logs from Lebanon and rebuilds the temple in Jerusalem (Ezra 3:7-11). Even today wealthy people line their closets with cedar, while others (like me) place cedar chips in their closets to deter moths and keep the closet air fresh.

The pillars of silver and the support of gold represent *wisdom*. In Bible days silver is ranked next to gold as a noble metal—unlike today's ready availability of silver. Though susceptible to tarnishing (silver much more than gold), both metals, when buffed, hold a mirror-like polish. Gold is extremely malleable and is prescribed for the most important furnishings in the Mosaic tabernacle (Ex. 25) and in Solomon's temple (1 Kings 6:14-35). Both go through extensive refining processes.

Silver is such a precious metal because of the depth one must go in order to mine it. The same thing applies to wisdom (Prov. 2:4; 3:14). Throughout the book of Proverbs the writer urges men and women to seek and obtain wisdom. The fruit of wisdom is better than are gold and choice silver (Prov. 8:19). Early in his reign King Solomon recognizes his need for wisdom. Wisdom, not wealth, solves the dilemma of ruling such a great nation as Israel.

The seat of purple represents *royalty*. The word used to describe purple, *argaman*, is a reddish-purple cloth—usually woolen. It is a borrowed word and probably means *tribute*.[48] The worth or value of an item is known by its vibrant color; the more vibrant the color, the more exclusive its use. God instructs Moses to collect blue, purple, and scarlet thread for the furnishings of His sanctuary (Ex. 24:4, 8-9). Purple fabric also is reserved for royalty (Judg. 8:26; Esth. 1:6; 8:15).

The interior is paved with *love*. The *interior* apparently refers to the inside of the chamber, closed off by curtains or panels. *Love* here probably describes the motif of the ornamentation on the inside of the litter.[49] In contrast to the portrayal of the external features that describe the central element—the interior—of the litter, the concern no longer is for the building materials but for the motif of the whole thing.[50] This particular palanquin is an extravagant traveling boudoir—a place in which lovers meet. The litter is defined by its purpose.

The object of these verses is to set before us the remarkable transport provided by Solomon for his bride through wilderness journeys. The use of these particular raw materials not only emphasizes the royalty of the occupants but the royalty of the wilderness occasion.

These verses may suggest, then, that the believer is carried through life onward to heaven in a vehicle as costly and glorious as the Shulamite's. The materials are the richest, choicest, most durable quality; yet surpassing all these costly materials, the inside of the palanquin is paved with love.

In the same way God's love testifies to women that, while passing through the wilderness—between this world and heaven, between the state of imperfection and glory—we have moments most gloriously spent in a most costly carriage, surrounded by a heavenly guard, and reclining on a beautiful couch of purple. A noted author compares this carriage to the Lord Jesus:

> In the cedar wood of Lebanon, we have our Lord's perfect humanity: fragrant and incorruptible. The silver speaks of His redemptive work, telling to all that He has redeemed us for Himself. We are His forever. The base is of gold speaking of His divine righteousness, without which there could be no redemption for us. None other than God Himself could effect our redemption. Its seat of royal purple speaks of His divine Kingship, His right to reign. Beneath all, as if it were the reason for all this lavish display of our Beloved's intrinsic value and power, is Love.[51]

As an observer the Shulamite steps back for a moment and charges the daughters to take a look for themselves at the King. Her Beloved—a KING! Her transport—a royal palanquin! Her protection—60 valiant warriors! All of this is provided for her—a simple shepherd girl. Heady stuff!

"Go forth, O daughters of Zion,
And see King Solomon with the crown
With which his mother crowned him
On the day of his wedding,
The day of the gladness of his heart."

The Shulamite once again expresses her amazement and points the daughters of Jerusalem to Him. This insight above all others testifies to the central truth of this new life in Christ: the Christian life is all about Jesus. This life is not characterized by laws and legalism but by worship and witness. These two activities go hand in hand. Worship without witness produces pride and a spirit of "holier-than-thou-ness" (Isa. 65:5) which drives people away. Witness without worship is legalistic at best and offensive at worst. Worship leads to witness, for one must speak of the majesty of the Beloved. Silence is not optional. Worship demands witness (Acts 4:20).

The day of his wedding, the day of the gladness of his heart. Women understand the joyful preparation for the wedding day—the dress, the bridesmaids, the flowers, the cake, the reception. Adequately preparing for a big wedding requires six months, with little for the groom to do except show up. No wonder the groom is so glad! With great joy the Beloved has taken such marvelous care of the Shulamite. He has spared no expense. He is extravagant in his love for her.

Three times in his letter to the Philippians Paul mentions the day of Christ (1:6, 10; 2:16) and cautions the believer to prepare for that day, so that it will be a day of rejoicing. His redeeming work is complete. The day of gladness is a day known only to God the Father. The Lord Jesus waits for the Father to release Him on that day to fetch His bride, who has prepared herself for the marriage supper of the Lamb.

Chapter 4

Behind the Veil

Since 9/11 we have seen many pictures of Muslim women dressed in their traditional *burqa*—the long, loose, enveloping garment that covers their faces and bodies. Wearing a veil is an act of modesty—shyness. Though many modern-day brides no longer are virginal, they still enjoy the show of modesty before their bridegroom. In the Bible we see many references to veiled women and to one man (Moses) wearing a veil. We also see God's purpose for the veil. First we will look at the veil. Then we'll go behind the veil to see just what the Beloved sees and listen to the couple's pillow talk!

The veil

- Rebekah modestly covers her face with a veil as Isaac approaches her (Gen. 24:65).
- Tamar covers her face with a veil as she deceives her father-in-law by pretending she is a prostitute (Gen. 38:14).
- Moses covers his shining face while he addresses the children of Israel and removes it while he speaks with God (Ex. 34:33-35).
- Ruth uses her veil as a shopping bag to carry grain (Ruth 3:15).

- The Old Testament has many references to the veil's being used as a symbolic curtain protecting the holy place.[52]
- The New Testament describes how the veil in front of the temple is torn from top to bottom as Jesus dies on the cross. This signifies that Christ, by his death, opens the way to Holy God (Matt. 27:51; Mark 15:38; Luke 23:45; Heb. 6:19; 9:3; 10:20). In Hebrews 10:20 we read that the veil—the curtain or entrance to the holy place—also is Christ crucified.

The Shulamite's unveiling is a vulnerable experience. She is exposed physically, emotionally, and psychologically. Unveiling her gives him complete access to places no other man has seen or been. Being unrobed for another is an exciting and frightening experience.

Some couples never go beyond the veil in their marriage; their relationship remains surface and defensive. Only as we develop relationships of love, trust, and mutual acceptance (the good, the bad, and the ugly) can we begin to relax and bare our souls to our partners. Inadequacies, insecurities, fears, and failures all create an impenetrable veil that obstructs the ability to receive love. The veil only is rent by a life laid down. Jesus—the ultimate lover and most intimate Friend—went behind the veil for you and me (Heb. 10:19-22).

The *veil* suggests a certain reservation in contrast to publicity; the eyes, as behind the veil, "would indicate a spiritual beauty that is not uncovered to everybody . . . to remain hidden until He pleases."[53] At Rebekah's approach to the waiting Isaac she veils her face. Can't you just imagine Isaac's anticipation as he waits for his bride's unveiling? The intimate moment between the Shulamite and her Beloved is heightened as he goes behind her veil. No silent observer is he; he graphically describes what he sees. The comprehending reader feels as though he or she is an intruder—a peeping tom, an eavesdropper.

Pillow talk (4:1-3)

The imagery is strictly oriental and goes considerably beyond the language we are in the habit of using in our day. Nothing is indecent, however; nothing is stated to make us blush in embarrassment. These verses describe the most rapturous delight the Beloved has toward the Shulamite. He uses metaphors drawn from his time period to describe certain physical attributes. "The resemblance in these comparisons consists not in any outward likeness, but lies in the views and effects produced in the views and sensations of the soul, in the pleasure had in contemplating these natural objects."[54]

"Behold, thou art fair, my love;
behold, thou art fair;"

First the Beloved speaks of the Shulamite's general appearance. Twice in verse one he says that she is fair. This is the sixth and seventh time in the Song he calls her *"fair."* In her own eyes she is anything but fair (1:6). By repetition he reinforces what he already has told her. He reassures her that, through love's lenses, his view of her really is the truth about her.

"Thou hast doves' eyes within thy locks:
Thy hair is as a flock of goats, that appear from mount
*   Gilead.*
Thy teeth are like a flock of sheep that are even shorn,
Which came up from the washing;

Whereof every one bear twins, and none is barren
among them.
Thy lips are like a thread of scarlet,
And thy speech is comely:
Thy temples are like a piece of pomegranate within thy
locks."

The Beloved highlights seven distinct features, which He has contemplated separately, minutely, and with great delight. Each feature is perfect in itself. "The minuteness of the inspection manifests the boundless interest and delight he has in her. The number seven, too, gives the idea of fullness and completeness."[55] What exactly does the Beloved's inspection of the Shulamite reveal?

Her eyes
"Thou hast doves' eyes." The dove is a ceremonially clean bird used in sacrifice and is a symbol of harmlessness, purity, and tenderness. In Scripture the eye is related to spiritual discernment and understanding. One Bible scholar notes that the dove has a wonderful power of distant vision. It supposedly can see, from an immense distance, its own dovecote (compartmented, raised bird house). When taken far from its cage, it ascends very high and steadies itself in the air until it has discovered its way back; then it flies straight and rapidly home.[56]

The Shulamite's eyes, exhibiting peace and tranquility, reveal the inner state of security as she revels in his love. Like a paper clip instantly moves toward the magnet, so the Shulamite, energized by love, draws irresistibly to her Beloved's penetrating, searching eyes. The eyes are the window of the soul. Her soul says she is content and happy as she stands before his roaming eyes.

I have known several people who are blind in one eye. The blind eye is obvious to the alert observer. The blind eye does not reflect or respond to light; it has no power of communication. Commenting on her own physical blindness, Helen Keller remarked, "To be blind is bad, but worse is to have eyes and not see." How acceptable to the Lord in the days of his flesh were those who gave evidence of having ability to see in a spiritual sense (Matt. 13:15, 16; Luke 10:23). Dove-like vision is a praiseworthy attribute.

The following verses depict the value of spiritual sight:

- The Psalmist asks God to enlighten his eyes, lest he *sleep the sleep of death* (Ps. 13:3).
- Jesus speaks to the people in parables as He fulfills Isaiah's prophecy; though the people have physical sight, they do not see spiritually (Matt. 13:13-16; Isa. 6:9, 10).
- Jesus uses the Pharisees and Herod to illustrate people with hard hearts who do not see or comprehend spiritual truth (Mark 8:18).
- Jesus warns that going through life with one seeing eye is better than to have sight in both while you offend a holy God (Mark 9:47).
- Jesus praises the Father that truth is revealed to babes while hidden to the world's wise and prudent. He pronounces a blessing on those who comprehend spiritual truth. Spiritual truth is revealed by the Father to the Son and from the Son to those whom He chooses (Luke 10:21-24).
- Isaiah sees God's glory and speaks of Christ. Jesus also prophesies that the Pharisees cannot believe because God has blinded their eyes (John 12:37-43).

- Paul, recounting to King Agrippa his conversion experience, speaks of heaven's light blinding him physically for three days. Jesus reveals Himself to Paul and then commissions Paul to preach to the Gentiles. Through his preaching Jesus would *"open their eyes, in order to turn them from darkness to light and from the power of Satan to God, that they may receive forgiveness of sins and an inheritance among those who are sanctified by faith in Me"* (Acts 26:12-18).
- Paul, explaining why few Jews are finding faith in Jesus, quotes Isaiah 29:10,13, saying, *God has given them a spirit of stupor, eyes that they should not see . . .* and Psalm 69:23, *let their eyes be darkened, so that they do not see.* (Rom. 11:1-10).
- Paul prays for the Ephesian believers, that God would *enlighten the eyes of their understanding* so that they would have spiritual comprehension and would understand *the hope of his calling, the riches of the glory of his inheritance, and the exceeding greatness of His power* (Eph. 1:18).
- The Apostle John describes the one who hates his brother as one who *walks in darkness, and does not know where he is going, because the darkness has blinded his eyes* (1 John 2:11).
- Confronted for their lukewarmness, the church members at Laodicea are counseled to anoint their eyes with eye salve that they might see (Rev. 3:14-19).

Spiritual perception is a must-have for the believer! When in my own life I sense coldness of heart and dullness of eye, I pray, *Enlighten my eyes, lest I sleep the sleep of death* (Ps. 13:3b). I need sharp and focused eyes that are quick to discern the precious and wonderful things hidden in His Word and alert to what is taking place around me in the spiritual realm.

In 2 Kings 6:8-18 Elisha demonstrates that ability. Syria is at war with Israel. One morning Elisha's servant wakes up and finds that he and the city are surrounded by the enemy army. Overwhelmed he asks Elisha, *"What shall we do?"* After assuring the servant that they indeed outnumber the enemy, Elisha asks God to open the servant's eyes so that he can see what is taking place outside of the natural realm. The servant's understanding of the situation changes when he sees what Elisha already knows by faith. His eyes are enlightened. Like the Laodicean believers in Revelation chapter three, we are in need of spiritual eyewash—spiritual eye drops.

The words, *it was very good,* announce God's pleasure as He evaluates the creation of Adam. Our Creator takes pleasure in sight. May we be more concerned to have perceptions and apprehensions that are valued in our hearts because of the pleasure which our having them gives to Christ![57] May the Lord give us doves' eyes.

Her hair

"Thy hair is as a flock of goats, that appear from Mount Gilead." At first blush this likeness to goats seems an unbecoming observation. Burrowes makes sense of this comparison,

> The hair of the oriental goat has the fineness of silk and is expressly observed by an ancient naturalist to bear a great resemblance to the fine ringlets of a woman's hair. The Angora species of goat is probably meant here. The country of Gilead was most beautiful and fertile and abounding in rich pastures and aromatic growths . . . The whole region is covered with groups

of limestone mountains, intersected by fertile valleys, and includes the territory east of Jordan, as far south as the Jabbok . . . Such mountain scenes were more beautiful when on their slopes might have been seen a flock of these beautiful goats lying down. The comparison of a fine head of hair to the long, silk-like fleece of such goats in such a scene was natural. Few things could be more beautiful than the sight of such a flock reclining on the verdant, balmy slopes of Gilead, on a clear, calm day.[58]

Using an expensive fragrant oil Mary anoints the feet of Jesus and wipes them with her hair; the fragrance fills the room (John 12:3). Her hair—her glory—is a simple towel that refreshes the feet of Jesus. Beautiful is her hair, yet not too beautiful for usefulness. Not only do His feet absorb the fragrance of oil, but her hair absorbs the perfume as well. Everywhere she goes, she is an aromatic testimony to the beauty of her Beloved's feet *(the feet of those who bring good news*—Isa. 52:7). Just as the scent saturates the woman's hair, so the scent of the sacrificial offering lingers on the worshiper.

Long hair on a woman, according to the Apostle Paul, is a glorious demonstration of submission. A covered head indicates a woman under authority (1 Cor 11:1-16). Addressing the woman's head-covering Warren Wiersbe explains:

Eastern society at that time was very jealous over its women. Except for the temple prostitutes, the women wore long hair and, in public wore a covering over their heads. (Paul did not use the word *veil*, i.e., covering over the face. The woman put a regular shawl over her head, and this covering symbolized her submission and purity.) For the Christian women in the church to appear in public without the covering, let alone to pray and share the Word, was both daring and blasphemous.[59]

Submission is the normal fruit of grace; it is a distinguishing glory to the woman in the sight of the Lord. I teach a seminary class to student wives. Many express deep concerns as they seek to follow their husbands into pastorates or to international fields. I continually urge them to make their trust in the Lord greater than their trust in their husband's leadership. God is big enough to correct their direction should the husband lead off-course! Even if he goes off-course, God will use the experience in their lives to teach them how to walk with Him by faith. Submission to your husband will accompany submission to God.

Abraham and Sarah illustrate this principle clearly. Sarah disagrees with Abraham and takes matters into her own hands. She gets the baby she thinks she wants before she gets the one promised; by the time Isaac arrives, she has learned to trust God to speak and lead through her husband. Even Mary, the mother of Jesus, has to learn this truth. After His initial conversation with her about the birth of Jesus, God always directs her through Joseph. (Joseph secretly determines to put Mary away, but in the middle of the night God interrupts him and stops him.) All subsequent instructions (trip to Bethlehem, Egypt and Nazareth) are given to Joseph. Mary has to trust that God is big enough to lead her through her husband. Her confidence in God is so great that she does not argue with Joseph about the next step. She does not worry that Joseph will miss God's will; God can and will make the way clear to Joseph.

Today submission in marriage is a big issue. Many women maintain an air of independence within marriage. Some have separate bank accounts and lack financial accountability with their spouses. Many women, against their husbands' wishes, are involved in religious activities or church work. Perhaps these habits have been adopted out of mistrust. My husband, as the head of our home, will answer to God for the welfare of our family. We don't always have to agree; that is okay. Having a grand view of God is vital. I submit, not merely out of duty, but out of awe of God's ability to use my submission and even my husband's mistakes to accomplish His purposes. I am confident that God is quite capable in taking care of my husband! Simply put, unbelief is the root cause of insubordination in marriage.

Her teeth

Americans are blessed to have easy accessibility to good dentistry and orthodontics. In my overseas travels I have noticed that many people my age and younger have only a few teeth. Because I grew up going to the dentist and have good oral hygiene, I have all of my teeth. Our esthetically driven culture makes dentistry a lucrative career as we straighten, veneer, and bleach our teeth. In the Shulamite's day teeth either rotted out or were extracted. Having a full set of white, straight teeth set the Shulamite apart from her contemporaries, as their smiles revealed gaps.

Her teeth are clean and of equal size like shorn sheep. The members of a flock of sheep—freshly clean as they move up from the washing pool immediately before shearing—have the same relative proportion. The Shulamite's upper teeth join the bottom in a perfect fit, like identical twins—with no gaps.

How important a full set of teeth is in the ability to chew and digest our food, both physically and spiritually! Many believers are spiritually toothless; they are unable to chew for themselves and depend on others to chew for them. Many have become Bible study and video series "junkies"—waiting for the next series or book to be released by their favorite teacher. These vehicles have tremendous value; however, they are seasonings—not the meal itself. May God give us greater spiritual appetites to bite off, chew on, and digest His Word for ourselves and depend less on spiritual food from another's kitchen. The Shulamite's teeth are compared to fertile sheep. Peter records the antidote to spiritual impotence or barrenness.

But also for this very reason, giving all diligence, add to your faith virtue, to virtue knowledge, to knowledge self-control, to self-control perseverance, to perseverance godliness, and to godliness brotherly kindness and to brotherly kindness love. If these things are yours and abound, you will be neither barren nor unfruitful in the knowledge of our Lord Jesus Christ (2 Pet. 1:5-9).

The Lord provides spiritual food in abundance—66 books worth! He finds pleasure when we find His Word sweet and consume it. Like sheep up from washing, time spent in the Word scrubs us clean (Eph. 5:26; Titus 3:5; Rev. 1:5). Ask God to whet your appetite for spiritual things. Jesus promises a gourmet banquet to those who hunger and thirst for righteousness. He says they will be filled!

Her lips and mouth
Her lips are like a scarlet thread; her speech is lovely. The Beloved describes the Shulamite's lips and mouth to communicate both the verbal and the nonverbal aspect of communication. The mouth is an external indicator of an internal condition. It communicates emotions nearly as well as do the eyes. They work together, yet one easily can contradict the other.

You have seen people smile with their mouths while their eyes cut like knives. The mouth can express horror and happiness, cruelty and contempt. It can seduce and repel. The lips can purse with worry or relax in enjoyment. Wilkinson beautifully describes this member of nonverbal communication:

> The force of the comparison here lies in the colour; the lips were delicately free from undue thickness, and of the most beautiful deep red. The Jews know no more beautiful red than the bright rich crimson here noticed as appearing in a skein of thread carefully dyed red.[60]

His description of her lips, compared to a thread of scarlet, seems to suggest the beauty of a piece as it relates to the complete fabric design. Though colorful her lips are proportionate to the rest of her face.

The lips of the Shulamite not are only beautiful, they also produce beautiful speech. Her speech centers on her relationship with the Beloved; not only is his love abiding in her heart, it is broadcast through her speech. The life that is sustained by spiritual food will be expressed by comely speech.[61] The Shulamite's speech is consistent with her beauty. Television and movies are filled with beautiful women whose beauty quickly fades as soon as they open their mouths and utter vulgarity. They speak from the heart. From out of the mouth the heart speaks (Matt. 12:34). The way we speak is a highly practical indication of how far grace rules us. Can our Beloved say to us, *"Thy speech is comely"*?

Just as the Shulamite's eyes, hair, lips and mouth give the Beloved pleasure, so, too, do our eyes, hair, teeth, lips, and mouth please the Lord. He is blessed by our spiritual insight, our submission, our appetite for spiritual things, and our speech.

Her temple

The temples are the flattened space on each side of the forehead and the upper parts of the cheeks. "The temples of the Bride—the place of thought—are compared to a 'piece,' a broken part, of a pomegranate. The fruit is delicious to the taste, and when broken it is a bright red color mixed with white. This may suggest modesty, or blushing, and reminds us of 1 Peter 3:3-4,"[62] in which Peter describes the beauty of the hidden person of the heart. A beautiful mind animates and brightens an otherwise average face. Mental alertness is a very attractive feature.

Your temples are like a piece of pomegranate. When fully ripe the pomegranate is a color mixture of yellow, brown, and maroon and contains multitudinous seeds covered with thin skin and surrounded by red pulp. Pomegranates are embroidered on the high priest's robe and are engraved on the pillars of Solomon's temple and on early silver coins. The thick-skinned outer rind protects the sweet, juicy fruit in the same way the veil protects the sweet modesty of the Shulamite. The bones of the temple protect the frontal lobe of the brain from injury. Perhaps this comparison alludes to the importance of protecting your mind—your thought life.

Peter admonishes believers to *gird up the loins of their mind* (1 Pet. 1:13). *Gird up*—this phrase occurs in the Bible only in this verse and is applied to the mind being held in constant preparation. It is taken from the custom of the Eastern nations who, when they had occasion to exert themselves (as in journeying, running, etc.), bound up their long-flowing garments by a girdle or belt around their hips.[63] The Shulamite possesses a well-girded mind! Her thoughts are centered on what she loves. **Our thoughts are love-barometers, as are our actions.** What thoughts run loose in your mind? If you were to broadcast them, would they be unacceptable to the

Beloved? What's running through your head?

We already have admired the facial characteristics that capture the Beloved's admiration. We have observed the Beloved's uninhibited freedom as he explores the facial delights of the Shulamite. She is his; what he sees is perfection. Let's continue our eavesdropping and hear even more intimate details.

Pillow talk continues (4:4-6)

"Thy neck is like the tower of David builded for an
 armoury,
Whereon there hang a thousand bucklers, all shields of
 mighty men."

Her neck

Does the Shulamite have a sizeable neck? The point of the comparison is not the size of her neck but that it is decorated with armor of victory. Her neck represents strength of character. David's tower is a place of defense—a place of strength. Without character, the head hangs down in shame. The experience of victory has a way of restoring dignity, uplift to the head, and a bounce in the walk. Deliverance, or victory, is equated with the height of the delivered one's head (Ps. 3:3).

The tower-like neck of the Shulamite, adorned with many jewels, symbolizes the trophies God has won within the land of Judah under the leadership of King David. The bucklers/shields of one thousand mighty men hang on the tower as trophies of victory (Ezek. 27:11). "The tower of David, built in layers, surrounded by shields, gives an impression of uprightness, of defense, of inaccessibility and an intention to repel intruders."[64] "The shields of the warriors associated with the beauty of the tower are a continual reminder of the recollection of the noble deeds and triumphs in which those shields had been borne."[65] Defeat has a physiological effect: the head hangs down, the eyes are downcast, and the face appears drained and colorless.

I often pray that the Lord would be *the glory and the one who lifts up their head* (Ps. 3:3b) for fellow believers going through difficulties. The Shulamite has been delivered from the life of a shepherd girl and transferred to a life lived in a palace with a King. Don't you know she has a regal lift to her head and a bounce in her walk!

Her breasts

The Beloved's description is getting far too intimate! Are you still with me?

"Thy two breasts are like two young roes that are twins, Which feed among the lilies.
Until the day break, and the shadows flee away."

Commentators offer three different interpretations of this verse.

One, the idea of symmetry is introduced in verse two (shorn sheep bearing twins) and repeated in verse five. "The two breasts speak of affections that are in even balance"[66] Unbalanced affections really are a deformity. Jesus sums up the Ten Commandments with, "Love God" and "Love your neighbor." They are inseparable parallels of truth. The Apostle John clearly and emphatically teaches that the one who does not love his brother does not love God. He says loving God, who is invisible, while not loving the visible brother is impossible.

Two, the two fawns feed at their mother's breast. Like the

mother gazelle, nurturing what is loved is natural. Our relationship with the Beloved must be nurtured. Coates beautifully gives insight to this description, The *"two fawns, twins of a gazelle"* set forth symbolically the tenderness and sensitiveness of spiritual affections. These are timid creatures, sensitive to any molestation, and ready to flee from it on swift foot. The Lord would have us cultivate and exhibit affections that are delicately sensitive—that are quickly alarmed by the approach of anything that is of the world or the flesh or the devil. The holy sensitiveness only can be preserved as it is nourished upon appropriate food . . .The fawns "feed among the lilies."[67]

When I think of the breasts, I think of the shoulder area. I have met women with chips on their shoulders; I have, at times, carried one. The psalmist describes this oversensitivity as being easily offended. *Great peace have they who love Thy law, and nothing shall offend them* (Ps. 119:165). From where does this "easily offended" attitude arise? A chip on the shoulder is a nurtured self-love—love for ourselves—our rights. Resentment, bitterness and unforgiveness are nurtured self-love. 1 Corinthians 13 is a wonderful exposition on what nurturing genuine love means. We nurture what we love.

Third, a woman's breasts are the most powerful visible expression of her femininity. This aspect is shared with her lover. Her breasts represent her sexual attractiveness—her allure for her partner.[68] I glory in being a woman. However the expression of my femininity becomes harmful when I draw the attention of any man other than my husband to my breasts or any other part of my body.

As a teen-ager I wore extremely tight and revealing clothing. I had been a born-again believer only a short time when I noticed a Christian brother staring at me in a way that made me uncomfortable. At that point I was convicted of dressing inappropriately. I went to the extreme and quit wearing trousers altogether. Responding to the Holy Spirit's conviction I immediately changed the way I dressed. The next day I actually quit wearing pants. Two years of pants-deprivation went by before I felt free to wear them again. I had no idea just how deeply the spirit of seduction resided in my heart!

Young women today shamelessly reveal their cleavage, their stomachs, and their upper thighs. No longer is modesty valued. Britney Spears and her generation have a powerful effect on naïve young girls, even those reared in Christian homes. Mothers first need to set standards of modesty and then instruct their daughters on modest dress.

Only the man who loves his wife becomes jealous when his wife is inappropriate with another man. Love is jealous. The Lord Jesus, our Heavenly Beloved, is jealous for our affection. In my Bible I carry a tattered index card where I wrote the following on April 6, 1982, when I was 22 years old. I asked God to make me aware of His jealousy over my life for Jesus' sake. He has been faithful to answer that prayer. I wrote the following:

I, Iva, have made a covenant with my eyes.
Does He not see my ways
And number my days?
Let Him weigh me with accurate scales.
And let God know my integrity
If my step has turned from the way
Or my heart followed my eyes
Or if any spot has stuck to my hands.
May my eyes be like doves.

Iva Gryner, April 6, 1982

On the back of the card I copied the words:

Who among us can live with the consuming fire?
Who among us can live with continual burning?
He who walks righteously and speaks with sincerity,
He who rejects unjust gain and shakes his hands so
*   that they hold no bribe;*
He who stays his ears from hearing about bloodshed
And shuts his eyes from looking upon evil
(Isa. 33:14, 15).

I jealously guard my ability to be intimate with my earthly beloved and my Heavenly Beloved. As a believer in today's world, I encourage you to do likewise!

Here are two important aspects regarding intimacy:

1. Intimacy requires vulnerability. Notice that his description takes place once the veil has been set aside. His inspection above the shoulders may have been uncomfortable but not nearly as intimidating as his inspection below the shoulders will be. How vulnerable the Shulamite must feel standing naked before the Beloved as his eyes continue their downward path. She does not hesitate nor withdraw from his exploration. Just as the Beloved explores the Shulamite through eyes of love, so our Heavenly Beloved desires from us the vulnerability of intimacy so that we, too, can be righteously appraised by Him.

2. Intimacy is to be enjoyed. Exhilarated by love, their intimacy is to be enjoyed until the breaking of day. The mountain of myrrh, the hill of frankincense speaks of utter ecstasy—the high of intimacy. These words spoken by the Beloved convey satiation—a filling up of intimacy's enjoyment. The Shulamite has no shame, no hesitation, and no hangups.

"I will get me to the mountain of myrrh,
And to the hill of frankincense".

While sex is the joining of two physical bodies for immediate and short-term pleasure, genuine intimacy is the joining
of two souls for a lifetime of pure pleasure. Sex can be had
without intimacy; intimacy can be had without sex. The physical act is but one expression of intimacy.

Intimacy's summation (4:7)

"Thou art all fair, my love;
There is no spot in thee."

By morning's arrival, the satiated Beloved summarizes all
seven of her characteristics with these words, *"Thou art all
fair, my love."* This is the final time in the Song that he calls
her *"fair."* Has she finally, with much repetition, believed it
really to be true?

Granny beads

"There is no spot in thee." She is a flawless beauty.
Nothing mars her perfection. She is perfect in his eyes, without spot or wrinkle or any such thing.[69] Paul urges the church
to be without spot or wrinkle and to be holy and without blemish (Eph. 5:27).

The word *spot* is from the word *spilou*, which means a
stain, figuratively in a moral sense.[70] Our English word *spill*
is derived from this Greek word.

Wrinkle is derived from the word *rhutis*, meaning to *draw,
contract*. A wrinkle is a piece of cloth drawn together—con-
tracted.[71]

Or any such thing is all-inclusive—no stain, no wrinkle, or anything of the sort.

Without blemish, amomos, spotless. In classical Greek *spotless* was used as a technical word to designate the absence of something amiss in a sacrifice of something which would render it unworthy to be offered as legally unaccused and holy.[72]

When a lamb was offered for sacrifice, it was continually inspected for several days before being presented as spotless. This same word for *spotless* is used in the following verses to describe the Lord Jesus:

- His spotless and acceptable offering cleanses the conscience of those trusting in Him (Heb. 9:14).
- His spotless offering redeems the believer from aimless conduct (I Pet. 1:18-19).
- His offering presents the believer faultless before the presence of His glory (Jude 1:24).

As I grew up, I had *granny beads*. So did you! That's what my mama called this necklace of dirt beads thread with sweat—the single row of collecting dirt hidden within the folds of my necks and arms. Every summer as I played outside in the Louisiana humidity, the natural folds and crevices of my little-girl neck became a *granny-bead* factory. Every night Momma scheduled *granny-bead* inspection to make sure the bath water dissolved those little dirt beads hidden in the crevices of my arms, legs, fingers, toes, and neck.

Wrinkles and fabric folds develop granny beads of silken threads of lint within their crevices. The lint line only is revealed when the wrinkle no longer is gathered or folded. Spots and stains are readily noticeable on the most used areas of a garment. *Spots* and *stains* are the more noticeable sins.

Sin is well-hidden in the wrinkled places. The Shulamite passes the Beloved's inspection in both the prominent and hidden, intimate places. David petitions the Lord to inspect him:

> *"Search me, O God, and know my heart;*
> *Try me, and know my anxieties;*
> *And see if there is any wicked way in me,*
> *And lead me in the way of everlasting"*
> (Ps. 139:23-24).

Let's evaluate David's five-part request.

First, he asks for a **penetrating search:** *Search me . . ..* *Search* is the Hebrew word *haqar,* meaning *to investigate, examine; a diligent, difficult probing.*[73] David requests the probing of his heart. The request is:

- Urgent—Examine me and do it now.
- Personal—David asks for God to search him, not his wife, kids, or anyone else.
- Righteous—David asks for exposure of what only God can see: the hidden motives, thoughts of the heart.

Second, he asks for a **purging test:** *Try me . . . Try* is the Hebrew word *bahan,* meaning *to put to the test by smelting or refining. Bahan* is used almost exclusively in the spiritual or religious realm denoting examining to determine essential qualities, especially integrity.[74] Part of the privilege of being God's people is that of being tested. David initiates this examination by requesting God to know his anxieties—his disquieting, troubled thoughts. God already knows them; David is the one who needs to know what God knows about him. He needs to see his thoughts from God's viewpoint.

The Refiner's test is a

- Test for gold—a separation of the pure from the impure.
- Test for good—an affirmation of the pure.

Adversity has a way of surfacing what really is going on in the mind and in the heart. Adversity doesn't add or subtract anything; it simply surfaces what already is there. It affirms good thoughts while it instructs us to eradicate corrupt thoughts.

Third, he asks for a **purposeful look:** *See if there is any wicked way in me.* The word *wicked* means *pain* or *sorrow.* David asks God "Is there any path I am presently walking along now (though it looks good) that eventually will end in sorrow or pain?"[75] The path may look clear now, but just ahead may be pain and sorrow. Do I continue on this path? Do I now give in to little indulgences that one day will become big, dangerous habits?

Fourth, David's request is a **preventive request.** Our lawn care is outsourced. Every spring the company sends someone out to apply a pre-emergent. When I asked what exactly that means, I was informed that weeds can be treated before they germinate and rise up. I like that. I need pre-emergent treatment. I need those pesky weeds treated before they germinate—before they spring up. Pre-emergent rather than post-emergent is the preferred treatment.

Finally, he asks for a **perfected walk:** *Lead me . . . Lead* is the Hebrew word *naha,* meaning *to guide, the conducting of one along the right path.* The writers of the various psalms frequently recall how God in times past led the people along the right path. This request is for far more than guidance; it is that God remain the leader and show them the way of righteousness.[76] His request is for guidance, with God's goal and not his own goal in mind.

• **Guidance**—Guidance presupposes a leader and a follower. His request reveals his humility. It says, "I don't know", "I need your help." David proclaims his dependence on God to direct him aright. *There is a way that seems right to a man, but its end is the way of death* (Prov. 14:12). Apart from God the wisest man makes the dumbest decisions. We are not smart enough to figure it all out. We need to be led by Someone much wiser—One who knows what is ahead.

• **Goal**—His request, to be led in the *way of everlasting,* tells us that David clearly understands that life does not end with physical death. To be unprepared for death is foolishness. David's one life goal is to be prepared for eternity.

Take a few minutes and end this lesson by praying Psalm 139:23-24.

Spots and stains are unbecoming on a wedding dress.

Let us be glad and rejoice and give Him glory, for the marriage of the Lamb has come and His wife has made herself ready. And to her it was granted to be arrayed in fine linen, clean and bright, for the fine linen is the righteous acts of the saints (Rev. 19:7-8).

Just as a bride prepares herself for her wedding day, we, too, must prepare ourselves for the day when we will be joined with the Lord's Lamb, so that we are not ashamed at His appearing.

A time to retreat (4:8)

My husband and I enjoy walking together. Three to five times a week we walk four miles. These mini-retreats bring refreshment to our relationship. We spend the first 30 minutes talking about problems and people; the second half is spent praying for those we've just shredded! It is quite healthy! We take our problems on our walk and leave them there. The minutia of work, ministry, and parenting are spiritually and emotionally wearing. Sometimes we just need a break.

The Beloved summons the Shulamite to go away with him. She has been invited to his chambers, to his banqueting house, to his banqueting table, to the clefts of the rocks. She has been found wandering the city streets looking for him. She has been with him out in the wilderness. Now he is inviting her away from Lebanon to the mountains of Amana, Senir, and Hermon.

"Come with me from Lebanon, my spouse,
With me from Lebanon:
Look from the top of Amana,
From the top of Shenir and Hermon,
From the lions' dens,
From the mountains of the leopards."

Amana today is the eastern part of the Israel-Lebanon range facing Damascus; Shenir and Hermon are two peaks in the *Hermon* range.[77] *Amana* means *covenant*. *Shenir* means *glistening*. *Hermon* means *lofty*.[78] The invitation to these three mountain ranges promises security (though lions and leopards roam the mountains), unsurpassed beauty unknown in the lowlands, and a perspective that can only be gained from elevated lofty heights.

The mountaintops are both a place of discovery and a place of danger. *"Come with me,"* he says, "to the mountain tops." He does not send her ahead and then promise to meet her there. No, they walk the heights together. He alone, who created the mountains, knows the mountains. Peaks so glorious and majestic, with their vertical winding paths and carnivorous wild animals, are dangerous to the unsuspecting. **The most beautiful places are often the most dangerous.**

When Stan and I sensed the call of God to go to Zimbabwe, Africa, in 1989, because of the political unrest the country was under a state of emergency. We went because we heard the Beloved say, "Come away with me." God does not reside only here in America; He was there also! Those six years were the most glorious yet most dangerous time in our lives. We were detained by the government and transported by military caravan to police headquarters. On numerous occasions our youngest son was sick to the point of death. He often was misdiagnosed by the doctors. He drank an entire bottle of Phenobarbital and spent three days in a coma. Toxic spider bites, malaria, automobile wrecks, and death of an immediate family member in the States . . . the list goes on! Never let the potential dangers deter you from going to the mountains with the Beloved. We saw people trust Christ, we baptized and discipled them, we started churches, and we trained leaders. We experienced great spiritual growth in our own lives. Our marriage is all the stronger for the experience.

Sustained spiritual highs are just as dangerous as are sustained spiritual lows. Both have enemies, but both have their places in the Christian life. As we develop spiritually, we are tempted to plateau and become complacent in our love for Christ, or we become proud of our attainments. Depression, resentment, distrust, and negative attitudes are enemies in the valley, as are pride and boasting on the mountaintop.

We just as easily turn down an invitation to the mountaintop because of known dangers as we reject the invitation to
visit the valley experiences of life. Dangers are everywhere.
Have you had a time in your life when you declined an invitation from the Lord because of the dangers/risks involved?
Wherever He calls is a place of covenant, a place of glory and
exhilaration, and a place with an elevation perspective.
Wherever He calls, He accompanies.

More pillow talk (4:9-11)

Here on the mountaintop the Beloved takes the opportunity
to reveal more of the depth of his love for her. Because of her
wholehearted consecration to him, the bridegroom is able to
reveal to his bride his whole heart.

"Thou hast ravished my heart, my sister, my spouse;
Thou hast ravished my heart with one of thine eyes,
With one chain of thy neck.
How fair is thy love, my sister, my spouse!
How much better is thy love wine!
And the smell of thine ointments than all spices!
Thy lips, O my spouse, drop as honeycomb:
Honey and milk are under thy tongue;
And the smell of thy garments is like the smell of
*   Lebanon."*

Twice he repeats, *"Thou hast ravished (stolen) my heart"*,
and calls her *"my sister, my spouse."* Scofield, in commenting
on this phrase, says, the word *"sister"* here is of infinitely deli-
cate significance and intimates the very whiteness of purity in
the midst of much ardor.[79] One look is all that is necessary to

unravel him. Her love is better than wine; her fragrance exceeds that of the most exotic spice. In the first chapter the Shulamite declares to the Beloved, *"We will remember your love more than wine"*; now he is the one who compares her love to wine. Both wine and fragrance are intoxicating; both arouse and play with the imagination and senses.

The Shulamite's sight, touch, and smell all work their magnetic power on the Beloved. Her lips drip as the honeycomb—an obvious metaphor for the sweetness of her kisses. *Milk* and *honey* are standard symbols for fruitfulness (Num. 13:27). The Shulamite's garments add to her allure; they have absorbed the fragrance of her surroundings—the wonderful cedars of Lebanon and the previously mentioned myrrh sachet that hangs around her neck. In Scripture *garments* suggest testimony before others—the outward activities and attitudes by which other people judge the reality of our Christian profession.[80]

The Messiah's garments are described as *scented with myrrh and aloes and cassia* (Ps. 45:8). Everywhere Jesus went, His garments were fragrant. This reminded people of heaven and healing and drew a woman with a long-term infirmity to touch his garment to receive healing. Our garments absorb the smells around us; when the odor is the sweet fragrance of perfume, people are drawn to us. In 2 Corinthians 2:14-17 Paul describes the believer, *Now thanks be to God who always leads us in triumph in Christ, and through us diffuses the fragrance of His knowledge in every place. For we are to God a fragrance of Christ among those who are being saved and among those who are perishing. To the one we are the aroma of death leading to death, and to the other the aroma of life leading to life.*

I once loaned some clothes to a church friend who needed them for a business trip. Until she returned my clothes, I had no idea that she smoked. My clothes reeked of her perfume and the tobacco smoke. How do our garments smell? Are we absorbing the aroma of the world or the aroma of Christ? Notice what Acts 4:13 says about Jesus' disciples, *Now when they saw the boldness of Peter and John, and perceived that they were uneducated and untrained men, they marveled. And they realized that they had been with Jesus.*

Smelly-Socks Tree

We are a fragrance to others—either good or bad, life or death. One spring day in Zimbabwe I awoke to a repulsive odor. We searched the house and the yard; we thought our dogs had killed a small animal and left it decaying in the yard. I had invited someone to arrive for tea around 10 a.m. and was quite cross when the source of the smell couldn't be located and eliminated. When she arrived, I apologized profusely for the horrid smell. With one statement she cleared up the mystery by saying, "Your Smelly-Socks Trees are in bloom." She took me out into the yard and pointed out the blooms and source of the pungent odor and explained how the tree got its name. Duh!

John said that the one who has been born again has His seed (1 John 3:9). When the Spirit enters our lives, He does not work with what he finds there but with what He brings with him. He first plants within us the life of the Lord Jesus and then goes to work producing His graces in our character.[81] To save us completely Christ reverses the bent of our natures; He plants a new principle within us so that our subsequent conduct will spring out of a desire to promote the honor of God and the good of others.[82] John states three things about God:

- God is Light (1:5).
- God is Righteous (2:29).
- God is Love (4:8).

If He is Light, Righteous, and Love (and He is), then certainly His Seed (the Blessed Holy Spirit) will produce these same characteristics. Light, righteousness, and love—latent in the implanted seed—sooner or later will erupt in the hearts and lives of those truly born-again. As someone once said, "You become on the outside what you are on the inside."

The one born of God has His seed and will produce Christlikeness. The one born of God will not walk in darkness (as a lifestyle), for it is not the new nature to do so. The one born of God will practice the truth, walk in righteousness, and love the brethren. The person's new nature is to do so. The greatest evidence of a true disciple of Christ is a new life (2 Cor. 5:17). He must change our desires and dispositions to prepare us for our new destination.

Though the Christian life is not a perfect walk, it is a changed one—a progressive one. His involvement in our lives provokes new practices, new paths, and new pleasures. We are either as fragrant as a cedar of Lebanon or as odious as a Smelly-Socks Tree.

Intimacy's refuge (4:12-15)

A garden exists for the purpose of bearing beauty and fruit. The Beloved associates the Shulamite with a garden. It must be tended and protected to be enjoyed. *"A garden inclosed"*, *"a spring shut up"*, and *"a fountain sealed"* all are "metaphors for the girl's privacy, her exclusivity, her sole allegiance to her lover. More particularly, they could refer to her sexual exclusiveness, her non-availability to anyone but him."[83] He planted the garden, he tended it, and he reaped the benefit.

"A garden inclosed is my sister, my spouse;
A spring shut up, a fountain sealed.
Thy plants are an orchard of pomegranates, with
*   pleasant fruits;*
Camphire, with spikenard, spikenard and saffron;
Calamus and cinnamon, with all trees of frankincense,
Myrrh and aloes, with all the chief spices:
A fountain of gardens, a well of living waters,
And streams from Lebanon."

"A garden inclosed"
Clearing new ground is not an easy task. Plowing unbroken ground is difficult. Building a fence is a task all its own. Trees have to be cut; stumps, brush, and rocks have to be removed. In the Zimbabwean rural areas the villagers used large broken limbs and wove them into barriers to protect their crops from animals.

"A spring shut up" and *"a fountain sealed"*
Gardens must have a stable and nearby water source. No water; no fruit. The water supply has to be protected from contamination. When water wells are drilled in Africa, the concrete cistern is encased with walls high enough to keep the out the animals.

"An orchard . . . with pleasant fruits"
The Shulamite's garden contains fruit and spices—fruit for eating, spices for fragrance, and herbs for cooking and for healing.

"A fountain of gardens"

A garden must be well-fenced, well-planted, and well-tended. (What is the source of all the weeds?) It is a "piece of ground which has been *picked out, purchased, protected* with a wall or a fence, *provided for* with water, *planned and planted* for a particular and personal *purpose.*"[84] Gardening on hilly terrain necessitates terracing narrow strips and hauling water. As the water, hauled to the top terrace by the gardener, overflows, it cascades and waters the terraces below.

"A well of living waters, and streams from Lebanon"

In 1982 Stan flew to Israel, where I lived at the time, and proposed. Several kilometers from the base of Mt. Hermon nests a communal farm, Kibbutz Dafna (where I resided), through which winds a cold spring fed from the mountain. By the side of this spring he asked me to marry him. As the spring continues its southward journey, it eventually finds its way to the Sea of Galilee. Decade after decade, century after century this and other streams from the mountain range of Lebanon feed this famous mass of water on which Jesus walked.

Everywhere springs flow, gardens are found. Transformed, the Shulamite is the rich beneficiary of the Beloved's love, as exhibited by his description in the aforementioned verses.

Intimacy's invitation (4:16)

The Shulamite:

"Awake, O north wind; and come, O south;
Blow upon my garden that the spices thereof may flow
    out.
Let my beloved come to his garden and eat its pleasant
    fruits."

Some plants release their fragrance as the rain and dew fall on them; others radiate with a subtle scent as the sun's warm rays smile affectionately on them. With stubborn refusal still others withhold their potent fragrance until forcibly penetrated by bending or breaking. This also occurs with our lives. Light rain, intense heat, and lightning storms are the varied experiences needed to manifest the graces of Christ in our lives. That a tree grows strong and sturdy when it is buffeted by contrary winds and storms is a well-known fact. The winds and storms drive the roots deeper into the earth where they not only find strength to withstand the storms but nourishment to develop beautiful foliage and fruit. The Shulamite invites the wind's release on her garden.

The *"north wind"*
First she calls on the *"north wind"*, *"Awake. Blow."* The north wind, with its chilly blasts, is not always welcome. Snow, ice, and wintry blizzards accompany the north wind. It drives bears and reptiles into hibernation. Frostbite, slick ice, and other wintry side-effects impose their curfew on the nor'easter recipient. For some it is a winter wonderland; for others it is retirement time in Florida. The north wind has positive contributions; mosquitoes and other insect pests die at first frost and chicken-noodle soup sales spike during winter. Chili tastes better, too.

The south wind
Then she calls on the south wind. *"Awake. Blow."* Dangers, such as hurricanes, tornadoes, and severe flooding are affiliated with southern winds. Flies, heat, and humidity are repressive companions of tropical winds. During the summer months lemonade, iced tea, ice cream, and watermelon reach their enjoyment peaks.

Isaiah compares rain and snow to the Word of God,

For as the rain comes down, and the snow from heaven, and do not return there, but water the earth, and make it bring forth and bud, that it may give seed to the sower and bread to the eater, So shall My word be that goes forth from My mouth; it shall not return to Me void, but it shall accomplish what I please and it shall prosper in the thing for which I sent it (Isa. 55:10).

Both accomplish their God-ordained purposes. Why does God send the wind on the unsuspecting believer?

- He sends the winds of adversity to make us grow.
- He sends the winds of testing to try our faith.
- He sends the winds of affliction, that we really may come to know Him better as Burden-Bearer.
- He sends the winds of disappointment that we may learn to trust Him.
- He sends the winds of changed plans, that we may learn to let Him make our plans.
- He sends the winds of chastening, that we may become more like the Lord Jesus.[85]

2003: A summer of storms

Several years ago as I prepared to teach this material at a springtime women's conference, I sensed the Holy Spirit prompting me to ask for the winds to blow on my life. His prompting was His preparation for what was to be a summer of adversity.

Three weeks later, during the final week of school, our older son fell during an after-school sport event and broke his arm. The next week our younger son fell on the school track. His lung collapsed; this put him in the hospital for three or four days. The next week we left for family vacation and had been driving for about eight hours when I turned on my cell phone to discover my voice message box was full. As I scrolled through to see who had called so many times, the phone rang. It was my neighbor. She said "Girl, everybody is trying to reach you. Your house is on fire." I could hear the fire trucks in the background. Quickly we pulled over on the side of the road, had a good cry, and drove through the night another eight hours. We were greeted the next morning by the shell that once had been our home. The corpse of our family pet lay on our veranda. Very little could be salvaged. The computer containing this manuscript had shriveled to half its size. I did find and remove my scorched jewelry box.

The next week our youngest son's best friend died in an ATV accident. We moved from the hotel to an apartment, where we were to live while our house was being rebuilt.

The next week the air-conditioning went out in our van.

A few days later I was sideswiped by another driver who demolished the driver's side of my van.

Two weeks after the wreck we received a letter from the IRS; we were being audited for our charitable giving.

Two weeks later Hurricane Elvis arrived in Memphis. This hurricane-strength, straight-line wind storm did historic damage to the city and to our house (in the process of being built). This necessitated a new roof and a third insurance claim in six weeks. For the next two weeks we were without power (in the hottest month of the year cooking all meals on a gas grill).

No sooner did we clean up after Hurricane Elvis, my husband and I returned from new-student orientation at the seminary to our apartment only to find that it had been burglarized. Only two items were missing: all of my jewelry rescued from the fire and the digital camera with all of the fire documentation for the insurance. By now I am stressed! Crying, I called a friend and said, "God's not letting me have anything!"

On top of all of this we were going through a family drama that threatened to tear us apart emotionally.

The apartment people scheduled a repairperson to rewire the security system. He arrived in the middle of my trying to get my husband packed and to the airport. In my heart I sensed the Lord wanted me to witness to the electrician. Time did not allow for a spiritual conversation before we left for the airport. Feeling depressed, I thought about going shopping instead of returning to the apartment. The Spirit would not let me. Arriving at the apartment complex I was surprised to see the electrician still there. After he completed his work, I asked if he had a few minutes to talk. At the end of our conversation, he trusted Jesus Christ as his Lord and Savior. Our lives would not have intersected had not our house burned down.

A part of me hoped that this young man was worth our house burning down. God reminded me that He paid an incomparable price for that young man's salvation. At a wedding reception a year later, a young man approached me and asked whether I remembered him. After a minute I placed him as the electrician at the burglarized apartment a year earlier. He told me that he had been baptized and married at that church. He was so excited to introduce me to his wife. Was he worth it? I think so. **Only eternity will reveal completely what the summer of 2003 really accomplished.**

The very things we shrink from are the experiences that will work in us to produce the peaceable fruit of righteousness. I've heard of a man who had the words *God is love* painted on his weathervane to remind him that whichever way the wind blows, God is love. Both the north and south winds have hazards and benefits. Both are necessary.

Chapter 5

Relationship Hiccups

We closed the previous chapter with the Shulamite's invitation to the north and south wind to *"blow upon my garden that the spices thereof may flow out. Let my beloved come to his garden."* She makes her request; let's see how he answers.

A fair exchange (5:1)

What a quick reply! *"I have come . . . I have gathered . . . I have eaten . . . I have drunk . . .."* These statements are written in perfect tense "describing his present enjoyment or looking back on his immediate past pleasure."[86] He finds in this garden all that his heart desires. These verses convey the idea of a banquet and of feasting on the most delicious fruits. Othmar Keel recognized the significance of this verse, "Eating and drinking are metaphors of the lovers' erotic pleasures, but that metaphor does not exhaust the meaning of these terms. Eating and drinking imply appropriation in the fullest sense. The object of a person's love becomes part of that person."[87]

The Beloved reminds us of the purity of their relationship by calling the Shulamite *"my sister."* *"My sister"* also suggests the permanency of their relationship. A sister is always a sister, whether she is single, divorced, or even dead. *"My spouse"* refers to the rightness of their intimacy. They are wed and belong to one another in purity and in a marital covenant.

"I have come to my garden, my sister, my spouse;
I have gathered my myrrh with my spice;
I have eaten my honeycomb with my honey;
I have drunk my wine with my milk."

Notice: a transition of ownership has taken place; her garden has become his garden. Nine times the Beloved uses a strong possessive *"my"* to show his passionate response to the Shulamite's invitation to *"my"* garden in 4:16. She is his *"garden, sister, spouse, myrrh, spice, honeycomb, honey, wine* and *milk."* Ownership: *"my garden."* Relationship: *"my sister, my spouse."* Enjoyment: *"I have gathered, eaten, drunk."*

(To his friends):
"Eat, O friends!
Drink, yes, drink deeply,
O beloved ones!"

Traditional wedding ceremonies are performed before witnesses and then celebrated with those witnesses. Wedding banns (announcements) are published, invitations are sent, and guests are expected. The taking of a woman by a man in marriage not only is an intimate private matter but also is a public declaration. The Beloved calls his friends to celebrate, affirm, and respect the exclusivity of the marital covenant. To the companions the ceremony and consummation testify that both bride and groom no longer are available to the opposite sex. Marriage affects all other personal relationships. Though the wedding ring has lost much of its meaning today, its wearing signaled to all observers the sacred and exclusive nature of the marriage. At its heart true Christianity is both absolute in surrender and exclusive in nature.

About love and the marriage relationships we see two truths:

First, love produces a willing surrender. The Beloved's appropriation of the Shulamite's garden isn't about conquering an unwilling maiden or coercing an invitation from her. She invited. He responded. He answered her invitation and found total and complete enjoyment. Just as the Beloved is quick to accept the Shulamite's offer to visit her garden and make it his, so the Heavenly Beloved quickly will respond to such a request from us. Just as the Shulamite is satisfied with the Beloved's appropriation, so the Lord finds satisfaction in a life completely yielded without any reservations. My garden is His garden, to which He has complete access and unashamed enjoyment. How amazing is the thought that we give satisfaction to the Lord Jesus! He longs for an invitation into our garden.

Second, love demands exclusivity. Both the Beloved and the Shulamite draw clear and unmistakable boundaries around their relationship: the Shulamite with the daughters (2:7; 3:5; 8:4) and the Beloved with his friends. All other relationships are secondary. Just as marriage changes the personal relationships of the bride and groom with their companions, so our relationship with the Heavenly Beloved changes and challenges our relationships with all others. Others can celebrate your marriage, but they cannot participate in your marriage.

When a third party causes the breakup of a marriage, the third party is accused of alienation of affection; this third party drives a wedge between the two. Alienation of affection between husband and wife can be attributed to putting the children, extended family, career, hobbies, or sports first. The relationship with the Heavenly Beloved suffers from alienation of affection when we allow our husband, children, career, or Christian service to have a place before this most precious relationship. When your relationship with the Beloved is priority, then He will ensure that you are a better wife, mom, employee, and servant in the church.

This idea of marriage changing all other personal relationships reminds me of the blind street-beggars in Zimbabwe. Blind mothers with small children camped regularly on the sidewalks of busy intersections. They depended on the handouts of the seeing and compassionate. Rarely would I give money; instead I would buy bread, milk and panties for the little underclothed girls.

I often wondered what the giving of sight would do for these beggars. Receiving sight would demand radical changes in all personal relationships. Begging no longer would be justifiable; a skill would have to be learned. Daughters would have to learn how to relate to a seeing mother, husbands to the seeing wife, and vice versa. Just as healing for the blind challenges all personal relationships, so the marriage of two people changes relationships and responsibilities forever.

A storm on the horizon (5:2-8)

We already have had one episode (in chapter three) in which the Beloved's absence produces a temporary separation, sudden panic, and a night of searching. It ends with the Beloved finding the Shulamite wandering in the streets. The first separation is because of the Shulamite's inexperience. The second separation follows on the heels of consummated love. The chapter at hand reveals a second and more prolonged separation, because the Shulamite rejects the Beloved's pleading request.

The Shulamite:
"I sleep, but my heart is awake";
The Shulamite is in bed, alone, half-asleep and half-awake. The *"heart"* is the first thing to awaken and the last to fall asleep.[88] Apparently she had waited up for her lover; because

of his lateness she had already fallen asleep. Suddenly she awakes to his knocking and his voice.

> *"It is the voice of my beloved!*
> *He knocks, saying,*
> *'Open for me, my sister, my love,*
> *My dove, my perfect one;*
> *For my head is covered with dew,*
> *My locks with the drops of the night.'"*

Though the Beloved is the crowned King, he is not sitting at his banqueting table or beckoning her to join him on the mountains. He is seeking shelter from the bone-chilling cool rain of the night. Her refusal of entrance bars him from his rightful place. On that late, rainy night he pleads with the Shulamite to open the door.

A closed door

A bar locks the door from the inside. He will not force his way in; she must be the one to open the door. *"Open for me."* He initiates, but cooperating by opening the door is up to her. He waits to be wanted; he wants to be wanted. His request is simple. No meal or warm fire is mentioned, though he probably is wet, cold, and hungry. He wants to be with her; he wants her for himself.

- His plea is seductive: *"my sister, my love, my dove, my perfect one."*
- His timing is inopportune (a late rainy night).
- His appearance is unappealing (wet hair).
- His request inconvenient (wet feet—hers are dry and warm).

What's with the Shulamite? Such affecting appeals don't instantly move her from the bed to the door. Her arms should have been open to this cold and wet groom. His appearance demonstrates his great shepherd's heart. Left to themselves the sheep would have been afraid and endangered by the adverse weather conditions. Driven by concern the shepherd does not rest until all the sheep are taken care of, regardless of the lateness of the hour or the cold dampness of the night.

Jesus too, stands at the door and knocks. Like the Shulamite, the attention of women today is given to personal comfort—enjoying the benefits of belonging to the King, yet not enjoying the King himself. *"Behold I stand at the door and knock. If anyone hears My voice and opens the door, I will come in to him and dine with him, and he with Me."*[89] This verse is most often applied to an evangelistic appeal, yet believers are the ones who neglect spiritual dining with King Jesus. Jesus is on the outside knocking, speaking, and waiting. He, too, waits to be wanted—wants to be wanted. The door opens from the inside.

The Shulamite's excuse

In this country not a shared bedroom exists in which tension does not occasionally or perhaps frequently lift its snarling head.[90] Every marriage has its ups and downs. Battles in marriage are fought over finances, discipline of children, or sex. Unequal needs and differing philosophies produce tension. Many times the differences expressed by one partner are not better or worse than the other's; they merely are different. Therefore communication and adjustments are required. Selfishness, independence, and a desire to control are only a few of the elements that produce tension in relationships.

Tension is necessary for growth.

*"I have taken off my robe;
How can I put it on again?
I have washed my feet;
How can I defile them?"*

Why does the Shulamite experience an attitude of coldness or reservation with the Beloved after longing for and receiving the King's attention? In *When Heaven Is Silent,* Ron Dunn argues that our toughest battle is with God. Love for ourselves demands that we be in charge instead of God. Having received such marvelous love and acceptance, the Shulamite simply wants to remain in charge of the relationship.

Was remaining in bed, where she is clean and warm, the wrong thing to do? Any other night, maybe, but this night her Beloved stands out in the rain knocking. In *Cries of the Heart,* Ravi Zacharias writes an excellent chapter on the God-created need for pleasure. He lists three principles which differentiate righteous and unrighteous pleasure:

- Any pleasure that refreshes you without diminishing you, distracting you, or sidetracking you from the ultimate goal is a legitimate pleasure.[91]
- Any pleasure that jeopardizes the sacred right of another is an illicit pleasure.[92]
- Any pleasure, however good, if not kept in balance, will distort reality or destroy appetite.[93]

Clearly the Shulamite violates all three. Remaining in bed, she is refreshed. However, as the Beloved's soulmate, she no longer has the right to deny him anything! (See 1 Corinthians 7 for the marital rights of husband and wife). The Shulamite's self-absorption destroys her appetite for intimacy with the Beloved.

The Shulamite simply is more concerned about the cleanness of her feet than about the need of her beloved to enter from the wet night. She is deliberate in her excuse. She makes her choice—"I don't want to be inconvenienced." **The opposite of genuine love is not hate but apathy and self-centeredness.**

Is this the same woman who begged the daughters of Jerusalem to not disturb their love? What is with her indifference? The bridegroom's advances are coldly rebuffed. "Not tonight, dear, I have a headache." Does this sound painfully familiar? Her excuses are weak and unconvincing. I would have to get dressed; my feet would get dirty (the distance from the bed to the door could not have been more than a couple of feet). Four I's are seen in her excuses. *"I have taken off my robe. How can I put it on again? I have washed my feet. How can I defile them?"* Self-occupation is the root of her lackadaisical attitude. She appears unwilling to put herself to any trouble, even for her lover. No longer responsible to her family to care for the vineyards or the flocks, perhaps she has become like the pampered "valley girls" of chapter one.

Remember the four temptations women face? Control, collect, compete, and complain. Here the Shulamite exhibits the desire to control her relationship with the Beloved. "I am comfortable; now is not a good time for me." Within each of us remains an unyielded room in which we keep a part of ourselves. To remain with clean feet in bed in this room is a lonely place. To surrender is to grow by giving when we ourselves have no need. Marriage is the mirror that helps us see ourselves more clearly. Marriage exposes the desire for independence, selfishness, and the need to control.

The Shulamite enjoys intimacy as long as it does not cost her anything and she can "call the shots." Now he is knocking, initiating intimacy, but she is unwilling and inconvenienced. As long as she initiates, she is in control. She is committed to his love but not surrendered to his leadership. A real difference exists between commitment and surrender. We can be committed to someone and still remain in charge. Surrender abdicates personal rights and authority to another. She is committed but unsurrendered. Many women approach marriage in the same manner. They have the attitude that the sexual relationship is something to be controlled, not shared.

Sometimes women approach in the same manner their relationship with the Heavenly Beloved. They are committed but unsurrendered. The *yes* is reserved until all options are explored and are found favorable. God's call is not a call for commitment but one of surrender. Commitment leaves me still in control—calling the shots and quitting if I want, while surrender leaves the Lord in control. We enjoy being loved and shrink away from relationships that don't meet our needs. Commitment justifies the way out. Surrender implies the yielding of all personal rights. Commitment is the loophole that allows people to quit when things become difficult.

The title *Lord* demands that *yes* be the answer before the question is asked. Perhaps the attitude of surrender versus commitment is indicated most clearly by the young woman at the missions conference who responded to the invitation by kneeling at the altar. Answering her father's inquiry, she simply stated, "I just put my *Yes* on the table, so that when He calls, the answer already is settled." The Shulamite has taken her *Yes* off of marriage's altar.

Regrets (5:4-6a)

"My beloved put his hand

By the latch of the door,
And my heart yearned for him.
I arose to open for my beloved,
And my hands dripped with myrrh,
My fingers with liquid myrrh,
On the handles of the lock.
I opened for my beloved,
But my beloved had turned away and was gone. "

Rejected and treated with indifference, he withdraws his hand and departs. L. M. McPhee identifies the key issue in her rejecting his request: "It has been pointed out by another, that the true cause of the Shulamite's declension here is a not a question of sin or worldly attraction but a separation of interest from her beloved's."[94] Her interests have become self-centered. She is more concerned with personal comfort than pleading companionship.

In the same way, do we recoil at the cross and its shame when He comes in His weakness? Our thoughts of Him, like Peter's, sometimes are offensive. In response to Jesus' prophecy about the death waiting for Him in Jerusalem, Peter rebukes Him (Mt. 16:21-23). Jesus embraces the cross because by it He redeems the world, but His followers—his lovers—flee from personal suffering.

Finally, the fear of losing her Beloved, who had spoken so tenderly to her, jars her from her stupor and arouses her to action. By the time she arises, anoints herself, and dresses, he already has gone. When the capacity is gained [for intimacy] but the opportunity for expression is stifled, the longing increases while the fulfillment waits.[95] With longings increasing and fulfillment enticing, the Shulamite arises and begins her quest of redeeming what she has lost.

"My heart leaped up when he spoke.
I sought him, but I could not find him;
I called him, but he gave me no answer."

Her heart was awake (v. 2), it yearned for him (v. 4), and it leaped at his voice (v. 6). The desire for personal comfort was awake as well and superseded those of the heart. Paul teaches in Romans 6:16 that a person is a slave to what he yields himself. Unwisely the Shulamite ignored the heart and followed the demands of her flesh. Wisdom conquers foolishness—I sought, I called, He *"gave me no answer."* Such is the result of trying to control the relationship and dictating when needs are met and under what conditions.

Rebuffed, the Beloved leaves. His absence exposes her selfishness. Repentant, the Shulamite is stirred to action. She embraces the sense of loss, rises from her comfortable bed, dirties her feet, leaves her comfortable bed, and seeks him.

A victim of circumstance
Verse seven records the severity of the Beloved's absence/silence.

"The watchmen who went about the city found me.
They struck me, they wounded me;
The keepers of the walls
Took my veil away from me."

What did the Shulamite lose? She lost the sense of his presence and the sweetness of their conversation and her veil—this veil was one of the gifts presented to a bride at her wedding.[96] She sought the aid of the watchmen of the city. Not only were they not helpful, they were hostile and abusive. She felt the blows more keenly as she realized that she herself had forsaken her protector. Had the Beloved been at her side, the watchmen would never have touched her. She was not rescued by her Beloved! Shocking, isn't it? Though he loves her, he does not rescue her. This abuse in the city streets does more in the development of her character than a lifetime behind palace walls (as we will see in chapter six) ever could produce. Abraham Lincoln and Mary Todd Lincoln's story is told poignantly by John Piper. Theirs was a marriage filled with pain. Mary Todd was a difficult and temperamental woman. She overspent and then complained of poverty. She was vain and flirtatious, yet exceedingly jealous over casual conversations her husband had with women. Abraham was aloof and often absent. Piper, asked how Lincoln could work so effectively with difficult people during such a difficult time in the history of our nation, answers the question:

> The long years of dealing with his tempestuous wife helped prepare Lincoln for handling the difficult people he encountered as president. Over the slow fires of misery that he learned to keep banked and under heavy pressure deep within him, his innate qualities of patience, tolerance, forbearance, and forgiveness were tempered and refined.[97]

He embraced rather than escaped the pain. Adversity in marriage developed the character which allowed this President to bring the nation through the civil war.

In the past several years several of my friends have walked away from their marriages simply because these women no longer were happy. Their husbands no longer met their emotional needs. Personal unhappiness, not adultery nor abuse, was their grounds for divorce. They deserved personal happiness, they said. What ever happened to the marriage covenant, for better or for worse, for richer or poor? Had Abraham Lincoln walked away from his marriage with Mary Todd Lincoln because she did not make him happy, our nation would be radically different today.

Just as history tells the story of Lincoln's difficult relationship with his wife, so Scripture speaks of the difficulties God's people have with their God—the seasons of difficulty and silence they go through as they react to God's initiative in their lives. Ron Dunn suggests that this subject of the "silence of God"—the "darkness of soul"—is unmarketable. The subject is avoided by believers, leaving those who suffer to suffer alone. Dunn then asks the question, "Darkness, despair, depression —are these legitimate spiritual experiences?"[98] Commenting on Isaiah 50:10, Dunn says, "The picture Isaiah portrays is that of a man on a journey, as he walks, the light is suddenly withdrawn and darkness rushes in. . . .. You feel alone, abandoned, forsaken."[99] This experience of silence, of darkness, is an inevitable and legitimate experience for believers. Dunn explains:

- God has a right to allow suffering and silence (Ps. 115:3).
- He has a reason for suffering and silence (Job 42:1-2).
- And He has a reward for those suffering (Job 42:10-17).[100]

The Biblical character Abraham experienced a 13-year period of silence. In fact, in his 100-year walk with God, Scripture records only 10 encounters in which God spoke to him directly. His experience can prompt believers to think.

Oswald Chambers, author of the popular devotional book *My Utmost for His Highest*, describes a four-year period in his own life in which he sought God and called out to Him but received no answer. "I had no conscious communion with Him. The Bible was the dullest most uninteresting book in existence, and the sense of depravity, the vileness and bad-motivedness of my nature was terrific. I got to the place where I did not care whether everyone knew how bad I am; I cared for nothing on earth saving to get out of my present condition."[101] He later describes these years as "hell on earth." Through this experience he derives much insight about walking with God by faith. We are the beneficiaries of that dark time in his life.

Suffering comes in different shapes and in different packages. In *The Hidden Smile of God* John Piper tells of the fruit of affliction in the lives of John Bunyan, William Cowper, and David Brainerd.

• John Bunyan wrote *Pilgrim's Progress* while he was imprisoned (12 years) for preaching the gospel. Quoting John Bunyan about the pruning process in the believer's life, "It is the will of God, that they that go to heaven should go thither hardly or with difficulty. The righteous shall scarcely be saved. That is, they shall, but yet with great difficulty, that it may be sweeter."[102]

• William Cowper, who wrote the often-sung hymn *There is a Fountain Filled with Blood,* as well as many others, "lived with bleak depression as a steady companion all his life, sometimes immobilized in despair, and repeatedly attempting suicide."[103] Though as an adult he was converted, for the rest of his life he struggled with periods of prolonged depression.

• David Brainerd lived a short life and at the age of 29 died of tuberculosis. After being expelled at age 22 from Yale, he took the gospel to the Indians in the New England area. Since that time his diaries, written 200 years ago, have impacted missionaries all over the world.

Each bore tremendous fruit that was cultivated in the different soils of suffering. The following poem compares the fruit of pleasure with the fruit of suffering.

I walked a mile with pleasure,
She chattered all the way,
But left me none the wiser,
For all she had to say.

I walked a mile with sorrow,
Ne'er a word said she,
But, oh, the things I learned from her,
When Sorrow walked with me.
—Robert Browning Hamilton

Victimization

Victimization in no way cancels out God's providential plan but rather causes it to emerge. Just as the oyster takes the grain of sand and produces from it a pearl, so God orchestrates something bigger from our personal pain, as we saw in Abraham Lincoln's life. Joseph profoundly illustrates this truth. No area of his life was untouched. He was thrown into a pit by his brothers, who calmly ate while they drowned out his cry for deliverance. They sold him to a traveling band of foreign traders. Though faithful in his new job as a slave, he was falsely accused and cast unjustly into an Egyptian dungeon. This dungeon of silence and solitude, removed from the previous dream of promise, was God's oyster shell of shaping Joseph into the man God promised he someday would be. The one consolation that turned Joseph's trials into triumphs was the continual presence of God, even when it wasn't tangible (Gen. 39:2, 3, 21, and 23).

Like Joseph, the Shulamite experiences disorientation. All her props are gone. Her circumstances surface the fear of loss, the fear of permanent absence, and the desire to recover his presence. Though uncomfortable, a period of disorientation is natural after loss; it is the bridge to recovery. What we do during this time of disorientation is everything. Giving up is not an option.

We want God to use kid gloves to conform us to the image of Christ. He uses the harsh experiences of life instead. Our greatest temptation is to draw boundaries around our lives that protect us from tough times and difficult people. Amy Carmichael penned these powerful words:

> God, harden me against myself,
> The coward with pathetic voice
> Who craves for ease and rest and joy?
> Myself, arch-traitor to myself,
> My hollowest friend,
> My deadliest foe,
> My clog, whatever road I go.[104]

Victimization is a part of life. We live in a fallen world in which fallen people do wicked things. Sometimes we are protected; sometimes we are not. Sometimes difficult circumstances are the consequences of poor decisions made. Other times they just happen. Children and women are abused. Cars wreck. Storms hit. People die. Suffering is a part of life—a result of sin entering the human race. Christians are not immune.

Much theological debate occurs over the subject of suffering. Joni Eareckson Tada enriches the understanding of suffering by stating, "Suffering is when God permits what he hates to achieve what he loves."[105] Jesus' teaching emphasizes the reality of suffering in this sin-cursed world. The final verses in the Sermon on the Mount recount the story of two houses. Each house is a life. The one house is built on sand and the other on a rock. The same winds, rain, and storms blow upon both. One collapses and the other endures (Matt. 7:24-27).

Suffering can be traced to two sources: the consequences of neglect and sin and the direct providence of God. In both cases love for self and its pampering must be thrown off. **Concern for personal comfort causes spiritual blindness**. The only cure is a withdrawal by the Beloved of His presence so that we may discover how empty life is without Him. Tada says, "Suffering bankrupts us, making us dependent on God."[106]

Seasons of silence and suffering effectively

- Simplify our beliefs.
- Discipline and shape our character.
- Cause us to shake off temporal slumber.
- Bring humiliation to unbending pride.
- Develop a deeper faith in God.
- Bring new discoveries about ourselves and God.
- Glorify God.

A penetrating question (5:9)

Quoting a seminary professor, Henry Blackaby says, "If you ask the wrong questions, you will certainly get the wrong answers." The question so often asked during suffering is "Why me?" The crucial question is, "What now?" Faith is not necessarily the power to make things the way we want them to be; it is the courage to face things the way they are.[107] The Shulamite takes a deep breath and declares to those who are most unable to help,

"I charge you, O daughters of Jerusalem,
If you find my beloved,
That you tell him I am lovesick!"

With her friends the Shulamite is transparent. She doesn't pretend that things are better than they really are. She says in effect, "Girls, I goofed. He's gone. Tell him I am longing for him; tell him I repent of my compulsion to control, of my selfishness, and my unconcern. I want him more than personal comfort, more than anything!"

Churches are full of hurting women sitting silent and alone in their suffering. Some years ago I was a member in a rather large Sunday-school couple's class. One Sunday I noticed the absence of a particular couple who had been faithful attendees. In the mall, when I ran into the husband of the couple, I was stunned to discover that they were in the middle of a messy divorce. No one in the class had a clue that theirs was a troubled marriage. I am very sorry that they did not share with our class honestly about their marriage and to seek help. Hiding behind religious masks of pretension is self-defeating.

On the other hand I can understand their hesitancy in sharing their troubles. Years ago I shared something in confidence with another woman whom I highly respect, only to discover that she had betrayed my confidence. That betrayal conditioned me to use extreme caution in all future friendships. I understood perfectly Jesus' warning to not cast our pearls before swine. Pigs and pearls do not mix. The betrayal taught me that some women are Miss Piggys and unappreciative of my pearls. Use discretion when you share intimate struggles. Reverently the daughters of Jerusalem regarded the Shulamite's acknowledgment and inquiry as a treasure, "a pearl."

A revealing question (5:9)

The daughters of Jerusalem:
"What is your beloved
More than another beloved,
O fairest among women?
What is your beloved
More than another beloved,
That you so charge us?"

Her passion for recovery of lost love provoked the women to ask a penetrating question, "Why is your beloved more special than any other?" "What makes him different from all others?" The positioning of this question suggests that it serves, at least in part, as a rhetorical invitation for the praise song (verses 10-16) to begin.[108] "Tell us how he differs from any other." Later we will marvel at her answer to their question. First we will formalize an answer to the "What now?" of suffering.

1. You are not alone in your suffering. Suffering is as old as is humankind. Bible saints and saints in every generation have suffered. Lost people suffer and have no hope. Suffering for the lost is as good as it gets. But suffering for those who know Jesus reaps great benefit. Psalm 119 mentions at least five benefits to suffering:

• We can take comfort from His Word (119:50, 107, 153).
• The negative consequences of wandering off prevent future straying (119:67).
• We learn more about ourselves and God in difficult times than we would if life were always pleasant (119:71).

- Afflictions bear the fingerprint of God and demonstrate His righteousness (119:75).
- We can rely on God to sustain us in our affliction with His Word (119:92).

2. Praying for pain's conversion instead of for its removal is better. Your suffering can be a catalyst to intensify a deeper longing for God. The byproducts of suffering are perseverance, character, and hope (Rom. 5:3-4). When I am in a difficult trial, I ask God to squeeze it for all it is worth—to thoroughly accomplish all that He desires to accomplish in me through trials. If it's going to hurt, at least make it beneficial!

3. Suffering intensifies our longing for something better. He hides his face long enough for us to discover how fervently and exclusively we want Him.[109] Suffering disrobes the triviality of materialism and crowns the eternal.

4. No packaged formulas or prayers will remove suffering. Unfulfilled promises by materialistic "name it and claim it" preachers have disheartened many. The Kingdom of God is not the Magic Kingdom. Our guardian angels are not little winged creatures with magic wands and magic dust waiting for the stroke of midnight to perform their miracle—to change our pumpkins into carriages. In his excellent book *Shattered Dreams*, Larry Crabb chronicles the story from the book of Ruth of Naomi, who endures 10 years of darkness and the death of her husband and two sons, with no hope in sight.

He records three lessons gleaned from her troubles:

- The good news of the gospel is not that God will provide a way to make life easier. The good news of the gospel, for this life, is that He will make our lives better. We will be empowered to draw close to God and to love others well and to do both for one central purpose—to glorify God, to make Him look good to any who watch us live.

- When God seems most absent from us, He is doing His most important work in us.
- Being blessed with the good things of life is not always good. Bad times provide an opportunity to know God that blessings can never provide.[110] God is not moved by our demanding temper tantrums. He is immune to our manipulations. He is not uncaring, but He cares too much to shorten the process.

5. Read the biographies of past-generation saints. Many have suffered before you; you can learn from their experience. Others' insight and perseverance will reward you richly.

6. Keep a daily appointment with God, even if you feel as though He never shows up. For months our youngest son once ate dry toast for breakfast every morning (no butter or jam). I was concerned that his day wasn't getting a nutritional start. The nutritional data on the side of the package eliminated my anxieties by listing the added eight essential vitamins. Oswald Chambers kept his daily appointment with God during those four years of darkness before he again sensed the presence of God. The Word sometimes may seem dry, but it is enriched with all the vitamins we need for the day.

Years ago, during the late 1970's, my husband attended a Bible conference in Switzerland. At an elevator he ran into Ron Dunn. "Living the Victorious Christian Life" was the teaching emphasis at that conference. Stan asked him to divulge the secret to victorious living. As the elevator shut, Ron answered, "Discipline, son, discipline." Discipline is not at all glamorous. The Kingdom of God is not the Magic Kingdom.

Early in my Christian pilgrimage a very wise man told me, "Read the Bible systematically. God knows where you are in the Word and where you are in your circumstances; He knows how to match the two together perfectly." For the past 25 or so years I have systematically read my Bible through annually. I have found that counsel to be true. The older I become, the more softly He seems to speak. I dare not miss a day in the Word, lest He show up and I not be there!

7. Suffering is an unavoidable feature on our pilgrimage map. You can make your valley a spring or a depth of despair. You decide. The following verses contain a marvelous promise to the one traveling through the Valley of Baca—the Valley of Weeping.

> *Blessed is the man whose strength is in You,*
> *Whose heart is set on pilgrimage.*
> *As they pass through the Valley of Baca,*
> *They make it a spring;*
> *The rain also covers it with pools.*
> *They go from strength to strength;*
> *Each one appears before God in Zion.*[111]

You can make it into a spring and be nourished by it, or you can feel sorry for yourself and starve. The Shulamite chooses to set her heart on pilgrimage and set out to find the one she loves.

8. Questioning suffering is natural. Give yourself a break! But asking the right question is crucial. The question is not, "Why am I suffering?" but, "Who is my Beloved?" We always end up on the short end when we ask or answer the wrong question. The Word enriches our understanding of God's nature and enlightens our hearts to our desperate need of Him.

9. Be on guard against your feelings; they cannot be trusted! Faith is sustained by reviewing what God already has revealed about Himself. The distance between the heart and the head is the distance from fear to hear. Fear is the product of an unbridled heart; faith, the product of a disciplined mind. In the midst of distressing times and circumstances the psalmist seems to look in a mirror, shake himself, and demand his feelings to stand at a salute,

> *Why are you cast down, O my soul? And why are you disquieted within me? Hope in God, for I shall yet praise Him for the help of His countenance* (Ps. 42:5, 11; 43:5).

10. Hope is kindled and progress is made when you see God as bigger than your suffering. When darkness or suffering overshadows your view of God, then you will become despondent and despair. Rehearsing His goodness and His character do not remove the darkness; rather, they address and disarm darkness' fear. The psalmist said,

> *I would have lost heart, unless I had believed that I would see the goodness of the Lord in the land of the living* (Ps. 27:13).

A silver-lined cloud (5:10-16)

Someone once said, "The stars don't need darkness to exist, but we need darkness in order to see them. We can be told of the existence of the stars, but only in the night do we see them. Just so, it is often in the darkness that we see God."

John Bunyan claimed, "There is more of God to be had in times of suffering than at any other time."[112] Suffering drove Bunyan into the Word and opened the Word to him. "Prison

174

proved for Bunyan to be a hallowed place of communion with God because his suffering unlocked the word and the deepest fellowship with Christ he had ever known."[113] In the same way the Shulamite's separation from the Beloved, her beating by the watchmen, and the stealing of her veil gave her something in return. They gave her insight into and appreciation of her Beloved.

Chapter four of the Song is crammed with the Beloved's description of the Shulamite's features. Only after she suffers heartache, physical pain, and the theft of her veil does the Shulamite describe the Beloved in detail.

Until this point in the Song, the Shulamite's focus has always been on what He has done for her: his invitations, his affirmations. She speaks of his fields, his banqueting table and house, his banner, and his chamber. Now she focuses exclusively on who he is as she gazes at his worth. She finally understands his value in and of himself. She moves from the gifts to the giver. Though absent, her memory of him is vivid.

The Shulamite:
"My beloved is white and ruddy,
Chief among ten thousand.
His head is like the finest gold;
His locks are wavy,
And black as a raven.
His eyes are like doves
By the rivers of waters,
Washed with milk,
And fitly set.
His cheeks are like a bed of spices,
Banks of scented herbs.
His lips are lilies,
Dripping liquid myrrh.

His hands are rods of gold
Set with beryl.
His body is carved ivory
Inlaid with sapphires.
His legs are pillars of marble
Set on bases of fine gold.
His countenance is like Lebanon,
Excellent as the cedars.
His mouth is most sweet,
Yes, he is altogether lovely.
This is my beloved,
And this is my friend,
O daughters of Jerusalem!"

First, she describes his general appearance: *My beloved is white and ruddy, chief among ten thousand.* Not only is he handsome, he is one of a kind—one in ten thousand. To her beloved all others pale in comparison.

Second, beginning from head to toe, she is specific in her description of his attributes:

His head and hair. *"His head is like the finest gold; His locks are wavy, and black as a raven."* Imagine a golden-sculpted bust with each facial feature caught in still life. His hair may be "compared to the fine wavy young leaves of the palm," his "locks full in flowing clusters, like waving pendulous branches, with curls rising above one another in profusion, black as raven wings."[114] If the Beloved is King Solomon, then Absalom is his half-brother; great hair runs in the family! Absalom cut his hair once a year. When it was weighed, it equaled the weight of two hundred gold shekels (2 Sam. 14:26).

His eyes. *"His eyes are like doves by the rivers of waters, washed with milk, and fitly set."* The Beloved compared her eyes to dove's eyes; she now compares his eyes to those of a dove. "The whole comparison represents the eyes as sparkling with vivacity, purity, and love of the greatest tenderness."[115] Light-colored doves stand out starkly against the backdrop of a wooded forest. His eyes are displayed like brilliant gems elegantly set in gold against a velvet backdrop. No need for eye drops "to clear the red out", as a popular commercial goes; the whites of his eyes are perfectly white. What she knows about affirmation and praise, she has learned from him.

His cheeks and lips. *"His cheeks are like a bed of spices, banks of scented herbs. His lips are lilies, dripping liquid myrrh."* The same delight that is found while exploring a fragrant flower bed is the delight she finds as she gazes at his cheeks. Hilly areas in Israel are often terraced with horizontal beds of flowers and plants. The flowers accent the rocky harshness of the hillside, so his cheeks highlight his rugged masculinity. His lips are like the fragile lily, distilling drops of myrrh instead of morning dew. Throughout the Song she enjoys the wonderful verbal deposits and the sweet kisses of his lips.

His facial features are symmetrical, like that of a well-planned garden. She never tires of gazing at his handsome face.

His hands and abdomen. *"His hands are rods of gold set with beryl. His body is carved ivory inlaid with sapphires."* Beryl was highly prized by the Hebrews. To them no illustration could be more beautifully appropriate for giving an idea of the finely formed hands, with fingers and nails of extreme delicacy, than to say they were gold rollers set with the beryl.[116] The sapphire is next in hardness and value to the diamond. His body excited feelings of beauty like those caused by gazing on a curious artificial work of ivory richly inlaid, even covered, with brilliant sapphires.[117] His hands catch the study of her eye, impressing her by their gentle strength. His body dazzles her by its powerful command.

His legs and countenance. *"His legs are pillars of marble set on bases of fine gold. His countenance is like Lebanon, excellent as the cedars."* The cedars of Lebanon are known for their uncommon size, beauty of shape, and foliage. "With perfect elegance and taste, the beloved is compared to Lebanon and the cedars for dignity and grandeur."[118] The correct translation for *countenance* literally is "the sight of him."[119] The sight of him conveys majesty and strength.

His mouth. *"His mouth is most sweet."* The Shulamite is alluding to his kisses as well as to the sweet words of his mouth. No book knowledge this! She has sampled firsthand the sweetness of his mouth.

All the comparisons of his attributes are rich and radiant in splendor. Summed up, the Beloved is altogether lovely. From head to toe he is perfectly majestic. He now is the absorbing center of the Shulamite's affections. Completing her description of the Beloved to the daughters of Jerusalem, the Shulamite exclaims, *"This is my beloved, and this is my friend!"* This is the first time she has called him her *friend*. Instead of driving her further from the Beloved, the Shulamite's beating and theft of her veil intensifies her pursuit, deepens her appreciation for the Beloved, and matures her as a woman. **The testimony of a maturing love is the depth of friendship between two lovers.**

The description of the Beloved not only stirs up the Shulamite's longing for him, it also furthers the daughters of Jerusalem's interest in him. Their conversation with the Shulamite piques their interest and provokes them to confess their own longings for such a relationship. In the next chapter we will study the Shulamite's influence on the Daughters.

Chapter 6

Love Suffers Long

Our response is everything! The silver lining of the cloud of the Shulamite's storm is not the answer to the "Why?" of suffering but the answer to the "What next?" of suffering. In *Where Is God When It Hurts?*, Philip Yancey sums things up well, "When something bad happens and we feel we have no control over the tragedy itself, we still have some control over our own resources. We can lash out in bitterness and anger against the unfairness of life that has deprived us of pleasure and joy, or, we can look for good in unexpected sources, even our apparent enemies."[120]

Joni Eareckson Tada, paralyzed from the shoulders down, says the turning point for her occurred when she found God as she let go of "what I thought he should be."[121] We know a God we want and a God Who is; they are not the same God. The turning point occurs when we stop seeking the God we want and start seeking the God who is.[122] The revelation of God to us is determined by our character, not by God's (Ps. 18:25-26). With Job she can say,

> *"He knows the way that I take; when He has tested me, I shall come forth as gold. My foot has held fast to His steps; I have kept His way and not turned aside. I have not departed from the commandment of His lips; I have treasured the words of His mouth more than my necessary food"* (Job 23:10-12).

Do you sense any bitterness or accusation toward the Beloved by the Shulamite? Instead of complaining about her difficulties to the daughters of Jerusalem, she amazes them by describing and exalting the Beloved. Then she solicits their help in finding him again. She has let go of what she thinks he should be and thoroughly embraces who he really is.

Though the daughters of Jerusalem initially compete with the Shulamite for the attention of the Beloved, their response to her dilemma is rather unusual. Unlike Job's friends, who condemn Job for his suffering and then question him to discover where Job went wrong, the question her friends ask, *"What is your Beloved?"* (5:9) ignites a resolute determination to answer that question. Because the daughters of Jerusalem ask the Shulamite the right question, "What now?", the Shulamite can face her suffering. She chooses to take a new look at her Beloved. After an intense review of his characteristics she chronicles a wonderful synopsis of her Beloved. Her response provokes the daughters to ask a second question.

An important question and a transparent life (6:1)

"Where has your beloved gone,
O most fairest among women?
Where has your beloved turned aside,
That we may seek him with you?"

No one enjoys being around a chronic complainer. People are driven away by the continued negative self-absorption of the one suffering; obsessive complaining wears people out. John Piper pithily observes, "Self-pity in suffering is the taste left after your sacrifice goes un-admired."[123] The Shulamite is not like that. Her response to suffering awakens in the daughters' hearts a great longing for a love like hers. Their hunger is exposed. They long for what she has.

"That we may seek him with you." The man or woman who has suffered much is often a redeemer-like figure to those whose lives are devoid of a close walk with God and whose answers only may be surface deep.[124] Like a magnet the daughters are attracted to the Shulamite during this most vulnerable time in her life.

"Where is he, this beloved of yours?" By giving a thought-provoking account or picture of her Beloved, the Shulamite successfully directs the daughters' attention away from her personal suffering. She paints such a beautiful picture of *him as he is* that the daughters are stirred to join her in her search. A lesson for us all, "You cannot commend to others what you yourself do not treasure." When we go through suffering without grace on our lives, observers gain a distorted view of God. Conversely, when we go through life's trials with the grace of God on our lives, others see and want what we have.

Observers ask those who suffer with disease and excessive heartache, "Where is God?"—not because they want a personal introduction, but because they want someone to blame. Theirs is an attitude of anger at the unfairness of suffering. Americans today impose on God their flawed standard of fairness.

First, we deal with the question they did not ask, "Why are you suffering?" Second, we will number the multiple benefits resulting from the Shulamite's trial. Finally, we will end the chapter dancing!

Job

Job's friends attempt to give an answer to Job's suffering. They challenge Job to look for hidden sin. They accuse him of neglecting the poor. They incorrectly assume that something must be wrong with Job. The picture, however, is much bigger than they possibly can comprehend. God reveals to Job His greatness as a creator and designer (Job 38-41). God then challenges Job by asking him 74 questions about His creation. These are questions which Job cannot answer; they establish the infinite gulf between the Creator and the created. Job confesses his limitations and admits that God is God and thus impossible for Job to understand with his finite capacities. The infinite vastness of God's creation stands as a rebuke to the finite and limited understanding of the created. Regarding Job, Ravi Zacharias comments, "What God wanted Job to realize was that this same God who brought such pattern and beauty into a world He had fashioned out of nothing could also bring a pattern and beauty out of Job's brokenness."[125] Because *"everything under heaven is Mine"* (Job 41:11), God not only knows but designs everything, including suffering, with a purpose in mind.

The first couple

From the very beginning suffering plays an intricate role in the lives of God's people. After Adam and Eve sin, Adam suffers the sweat of his brow to provide food for the needs of his family. Eve bears children through the pain of childbirth. The world immediately ceases being a place of endless joy and holy pleasure. God no longer walks with His creation— humanity—in the cool of the day. An animal is killed to provide a covering for the naked couple. Cain kills Abel in a fit of jealousy. Cain is cursed by God. Again and again the Bible records the wicked acts of sinful people and the painful consequences—centuries of human suffering. God's people are not immune. Sin and suffering in the world exist as surely as the sun rises and sets. The Bible is replete with examples.

Joseph

As we see in the previous chapter Joseph suffers unfairly. Genesis chapter 37 records the story of his brothers' treachery; chapter 39 tells of his false arrest and imprisonment. In spite of these horrendous events, Joseph perseveres. To preserve the lives of Joseph's family, God uses the evil plans of his brothers to bring him to the second-highest position in Egypt. We have the end of the story; Joseph does not! While Joseph is imprisoned, he has no idea the direction his life is taking. God is honored by Joseph's trust.

Blaming a poor view of God on the imperfections of a past dysfunctional home and poor parenting, especially by the father, is popular. Joseph's father has two wives; each has several children. Each wife has concubines who birth children to Jacob. Jacob has a rotten relationship with his in-laws. Joseph has only one thing going for him; he is his father's favorite son. All 10 of his half-brothers hate him and conspire to sell him into slavery. He suffers; even his dad is unable to protect him!

God's lack of intervention during suffering forces us to build spiritual muscle. Many Americans, obsessed with being physically fit, follow rigorous exercise programs and in the process endure a lot of pain. But in the spiritual realm they want the kid-glove treatment; they want God to pamper them. Just as we have no shortcuts to being physically buff, we have no magic pills producing spiritual buffness. Philip Yancey employs the following illustration:

A father determined to exclude all pain from his beloved daughter's life would never allow her to take a step. She might fall down! Instead, he picks her up and carries her wherever she goes or pushes her in a carriage. Over time such a pampered child will become an invalid.[126]

On this particular morning I am reminded of how we Americans insist on a clean, tidy little world where everything is black and white and we are in control. A normal fall day disposes brittle but colorful leaves in a blanket on the ground. With their leaf-blowers neighbors on both sides have drawn distinct lines between my yard and theirs. The leaves are admired as long as they remain attached to the tree limbs. Once fallen these leaves become a nuisance to be raked and discarded. The fall season bears much beauty—beauty accompanied with problems—as does life. We want life clean and tidy; things don't happen that way.

Philip Yancey lists the following 10 "advantages" to suffering.[127] My applications to the Shulamite are italicized.

1. Suffering, the great equalizer, brings people to a place where they may realize their urgent need for redemption. *Though the Shulamite comfortably has made the transition from shepherd girl to the Beloved's wife, her new status does not make her immune to difficulty. By suffering loss she is disturbed from her apathy.*

2. Those who suffer know not only their dependence on God and on healthy people but also their interdependence with one another. *As she searches the Shulamite seeks the aid of the daughters of Jerusalem.*

3. Those who suffer rest their security not on things, which often cannot be enjoyed and may soon be taken away, but rather on people. *Comfort and cleanliness are quickly discarded when compared to the worth of intimacy with the Beloved.*

4. Those who suffer have no exaggerated sense of their own importance and no exaggerated need of privacy. Suffering humbles the proud. *The dark of the night does not prohibit the Shulamite from searching for the one she loves. She endures*

the brutality of the watchmen and the loss of her veil. Not only does she have to leave the comfort of her bed in order to find him, she has to leave the palace.

5. Those who suffer expect little from competition and much from cooperation. *The Shulamite's passionate search is not crippled by her pride before the daughters in pretending that things are well. She needs them!*

6. Those who suffer can distinguish between necessities and luxuries. *Comfort and material blessings are luxuries. The Shulamite discovers that she much rather would have the Benefactor than she would the blessings.*

7. Those who suffer are taught patience—often a kind of dogged patience born of acknowledged dependence. *The Shulamite responds admirably to the difficulties she faces as she seeks the Beloved. She does not quit when the way becomes difficult and even abusive.*

8. Suffering teaches the difference between valid fears and exaggerated fears. *The loss of comfort and cleanliness is much preferred to the loss of intimacy. She is less afraid of the dark, the watchmen, and losing her veil than she is of losing her close relationship with the Beloved.*

9. To those who suffer the gospel sounds like good news and not like a threat or a scolding. It offers hope and comfort. *The Shulamite had become self-absorbed and pampered. Horrified by her apathy and the empty bed she does not lie in bed and feel sorry for herself but throws off the covers of personal safety and self-love and runs to find her Beloved.*

10. Those who suffer can respond to the call of the gospel with a certain abandonment and uncomplicated totality because they have so little to lose and are ready for anything. *She remembers her roots—those shepherd fields and vineyards and everything the Beloved has done for her—the joy of intimacy, the love they have shared, and finds leaving the palatial*

comfort and hitting the streets to look for the one she loves not to be difficult. Nothing deters her—the beating, the stealing of her veil—nothing.

The Song of Songs is the Shulamite's under-construction site. Have you ever noticed a construction site? Typically the site is enclosed by temporary fencing. A sign containing a picture of the proposed building and a construction company's advertisement are placed out front. The sign is a reminder to inconvenienced observers that the building one day will be completed—that the traffic jams and waiting created by dump trucks and concrete trucks, the noise, and most of all the dirt, will have been worth it. While the world hides the process and focuses on the end product, God's kingdom reverses this mindset. To God the process is as important as the end result. You need one to have the other. The Song isn't so much about the end result of finding love and fulfillment as it is about the process.

The Song of Songs hides nothing but openly describes the process or progression of the lovers' relationship. We learn that their relationship has its painful moments and is profitable and public; it would not be so painful if others were not always watching (If only He would conform me into the image of Christ privately, away from prying eyes). This is no different than the Christian life is. Let's look at the parallels.

A progressive relationship

From beginning to end let us follow the progression in her relationship with the Beloved beginning with,
"Tell me, O you whom I love, where you feed your flock, where you make it rest at noon, for why should I be as one who veils herself by the flock of your companions?" (1:7).

We find the Shulamite:
- Following—*"in the footsteps of the flock, and feed your little goats beside the shepherds' tents"* (1:8).
- Dining—at the king's table (1:12).
- Enjoying his pleasures—*"our bed is green,"* *"the beams of our houses are cedar, and our rafters of fir"* (1:16-17).
- Sitting—*"I sat down in his shade with great delight"* (2:3).
- Eating—*"He brought me to the banqueting house"* (2:4).
- Being pursued—*"Behold, he comes leaping upon the mountains, skipping upon the hills"* (2:8).
- Vacationing—*"Rise up, my love, my fair one, and come away"* (2:10, 13).
- Visiting—the home of her mother (3:4).
- Missing him—unable to find him in the city (3:2).
- Laboring—together in her garden (5:16, 6:1).
- Abandoned—beaten up in the city as she searches for her Beloved (5:7).
- Traveling—in the fields, the villages (7:11-12).
- Recovering—coming up from the wilderness (8:5).

The brief suffering in chapter three and the more prolonged and painful suffering in chapter five are just as important in the Shulamite's relationship with the Beloved as is the intimacy we find in chapters four and six. The eight relatively brief chapters of the Song abound with forward movement and increasing activity.

A public relationship
A construction site is an observation site. The life under construction changes from day to day as progress is made. The observer can see the progress, visualize the approaching com-

pletion, and endure the inconveniences of detours and dirt and be encouraged. The lovers' relationship is played out before the daughters of Jerusalem, her family, his family, and his companions.

Everything we know about Jesus, we know because it was done in public.

- John the Baptist announces Jesus as the Lamb of God at the baptismal waters (John 1:29-34).
- Jesus' first miracle is done in plain view at a wedding party (John 2:1-10).
- Jesus cleanses the temple in the middle of the day, when the temple is most crowded (John 2:13-16).
- The pool of Bethesda is crowded with the infirm when Jesus chooses to heal the man who has been crippled 38 years (John 5:3-8).
- Jesus feeds the five thousand with five barley loaves and a few fish (John 6:1-14).
- Caught in adultery, a woman is brought before Jesus and other worshipers (John 8:1-12).
- Jesus' betrayal, arrest and crucifixion all are public events.
- Peter denies Jesus and is restored by Jesus publicly.
- The believer is commanded to confess Christ publicly.
- King Agrippa is challenged by the words of Paul regarding the gospel, *since this thing was not done in a corner* (Acts. 26:26).
- The Bible is a record of God and His public works from creation to the consummation of the ages. God works in the public arena!

A profitable relationship

The capacity to know the Beloved and herself more intimately is enlarged by difficulty. Look at the progression of her startling insight:

- "*I am the rose of Sharon, and the lily of the valleys*" (2:1).
- "*My beloved is mine, and I am his*" (2:16a).
- "*I am my beloved's and my beloved is mine*" (6:3).
- "*Before I was even aware, my soul had made me as the chariots of my noble people*" (6:12).
- "*I am my beloved's, and his desire is toward me*" (7:10).
- "*I am a wall, and my breasts like towers; Then I became in his eyes as one who found peace*" (8:10).

Even the daughters of Jerusalem are now describing the Shulamite as the fairest among women (6:1). In a comment on Romans 8:22 Larry Crabb says, "The fondest dream of the universe is to catch a glimpse of real sons and daughters of God." Psalm 40:1-3 captures this thought well:

I waited patiently for the Lord;
And He inclined to me,
And heard my cry.
He also brought me up out of a horrible pit,
Out of the miry clay,
And set my feet upon a rock,
And established my steps.
He has put a new song in my mouth—
Praise to our God;
Many shall see it and fear,
And will trust in the Lord.

Out of the overflow of your walk with God, you minister to others. Piper says it best, "Suffering displays to others the supremacy of His worth above all treasures", and, "Whenever something is of tremendous value to you and you cherish its beauty or power or uniqueness, you want to draw others attention to it and awaken in them the same joy." Because this is the Shulamite's response, she has great influence with many others.

- The daughters of Jerusalem are awakened to their deep desire to know such love (6:1).
- The Beloved's friends admire the maturity which now marks her life (6:13).
- A relative is amazed by the Shulamite's appearance as she now leans on her Beloved (8:5).
- Her own companions and her Beloved are mesmerized by her voice (8:13).

The public work of God is profitable—and provoking; it solicits a response from others. In the secret, private place we don't mind being conformed to the image of Christ. But when we are in the public view, the world catches a tiny glimpse of what we one day will be in completion.

A painful relationship
The Singer does not record how long the Beloved's absence lasts. The first incident of absence in chapter three indicates the time is brief (3:4). The absence in chapter five appears to last much longer.

Ephraim: the fruit of suffering
The Bible is replete with stories of those who go through lengthy trials. Abraham waits 25 years for the impossible (two

old people to have a son) to finally happen. Joseph is sold into slavery at the age of 17 and spends 13 years in slavery and prison as God fulfills His purposes for his life. After his prison release and during the seven years of prosperity Joseph has two sons. He explains the naming of his second-born son *Ephraim* by saying, *It is because God has made me fruitful in the land of my suffering.*[128] The finger of God is the paintbrush and suffering the paint that captures the wisdom of God on canvas through the portraits of men and women of faith which are framed on the hallway of time.

Peter limits the time of suffering to *a while* and encourages the believer to endure. In 1 Peter 5:10 he lists the following benefits to suffering. God's goal through suffering is to perfect, establish, strengthen, and settle the believer.

- *Perfect*—to make a perfect fit, suitable, such as one should be, deficient in no part.[129]
- *Establish*—to make steadfast in mind, confirm, strengthen.[130]
- *Strengthen*—to reinforce, brace, or fortify. This word is better understood by looking at its antonym, which means to exhaust, to make weak or tired.[131]
- *Settle*—to found, to lay the foundation of anything; to ground, establish, confirm.[132]

Suffering does for the believer what success, pleasure, health, and wealth cannot do; it matures. In Psalm 13 the psalmist asks God five questions during his season of silence and suffering:

- How long will this last?
- Will you forget me forever?
- How long will you hide your face from me?

- How long shall I take counsel in my soul, having sorrow in my heart daily?
- How long will my enemy be exalted over me?

In the midst of trouble he asked God to enlighten his eyes, lest he sleep the sleep of death (verse 3). He then resolves to:
- Trust in God's mercy,
- Rejoice in God's salvation,
- Sing to the Lord because He has dealt bountifully with him (verses 5-6).

Paul promises those who are in trouble,

Blessed be the God and Father of our Lord Jesus Christ, the Father of mercies and God of all comfort, who comforts us in all our tribulation that we may be able to comfort those who are in any trouble, with the comfort with which we ourselves are comforted by God. For as the sufferings of Christ abound in us, so our consolation also abounds through Christ. Now if we are afflicted, it is for your consolation and salvation, which is effective for enduring the same sufferings which we also suffer. Or if we are comforted, it is for your consolation and salvation. And our hope for you is steadfast, because we know that as you are partakers of the sufferings, so also you will partake of the consolation.[133]

God offers consolation to the suffering believer; He is the God of all comfort. A poetic reminder:
Pressed out of measure and pressed to all length,
Pressed so intently, it seems beyond strength.
Pressed in the body, and pressed in the soul,

Pressed in the mind till the dark surges roll.
Pressure by foes and pressure by friends,
Pressure on pressure till life nearly ends.
Pressed into knowing no helper but God,
Pressed into loving the staff and the rod.
Pressed into liberty where nothing clings,
Pressed into faith for impossible things.
Pressed into living a life for the Lord,
Pressed into living a Christ-life outpoured.[134]

A second honeymoon (6:2-9)

When she has found Him, the finding is all the sweeter for
the long seeking. The following verses indicate such a renewal
between the Song's lovers.

The Shulamite:
My beloved has gone to his garden,
To the beds of spices,
To feed his flock in the gardens,
And to gather lilies.
I am my beloved's,
And my beloved is mine.
He feeds his flock among the lilies.

These two verses pose difficulties for most commentators.
They may represent her conscience-stricken recollection of her
lover's approach to her bed (5:2f) and her refusal to accept
him. Now she remembers their relationship and commitment
to each other.[135] Here among the lilies and spice beds, in the
garden the two lovers find each other again.

In chapter 2:16 she states, *"My beloved is mine, and I am his. He feeds the flocks among the lilies."* The reversal of ownership indicates the shift in the Shulamite's focus. Not *"mine"* first but *"his"* first. *"I am my beloved's, and my beloved is mine. He feeds his flocks among the lilies."* Notice the change? Before, their relationship focuses primarily on who he is to her—what he has done for her. His absence and her abuse and loss change her perspective. Even while they are separated, she knows she still is the object of his love. Previously his claim to her is secondary to her claim to him. Now they equally enjoy their claims on each other. Hudson Taylor comments,

> No sooner has she uttered these rightful words and acknowledged herself as His rightful possession—a claim which she had practically repudiated when she kept him barred out—than her bridegroom Himself appears: and with no upbraiding word, but in tenderest love, tells her how beautiful she is in His eyes, and speaks her praise to the daughters of Jerusalem.[136]

The second honeymoon begins with the Shulamite's surrender to his rightful place in their relationship. In turn his adoration of his Shulamite is breathtaking.

The Beloved
"O my love, you are as beautiful as Tirzah,
Lovely as Jerusalem,
Awesome as an army with banners!"

The very name of *"Tirzah"*—delight—speaks the beauty of its scenery. This city is mentioned in Joshua 7:24 as remarkable for its elegance; after the revolt of Rehoboam it is chosen as the royal city and preserves its preeminence until Omri founds Samaria.[137] The site is one of great natural beauty with extensive gardens and groves encouraged by its abundant water supply (one of the best in Israel).[138] In an almost worshipful manner he compares the Shulamite to the two most holy cities of his region.

"Awesome as an army with banners." As a military army lined up in battle array, majestic under its banners, imposing in its might, so the Beloved sees the Shulamite. Stronger from the trial of separation, she now possesses much more than physical beauty—beauty that is tempered by dignity, grace, and strength. His love for her is amplified. Though she has been neglectful in the past, the love of the Beloved remains strong. Ravished of heart, he now is overcome with admiration: *"Turn your eyes away from me, for they have overcome [overwhelmed] me."*

Hit the replay button (6:5b-7)

Let's rewind the tape. With little variation the Beloved repeats an earlier declaration (4:1-3). The Beloved's purpose seems to be to assure the Shulamite that from his point of view nothing has changed. By this repetition he assures her heart that her beauty in His sight is unimpaired by what she has suffered. Though he says nothing about her barred door, these expressions of His unchanged admiration of her now take a deeper hold on her heart than before.[139] What reassurance!

> *"Your hair is like a flock of goats*
> *Going down from Gilead.*
> *Your teeth are like a flock of sheep*
> *Which have come up from the washing;*
> *Every one bears twins,*

And none of them is barren among them.
Like a piece of pomegranate
Are your temples behind your veil"

In his descriptions of the Shulamite, he is never short of words. Every glimpse of the Shulamite inspires yet more descriptions—even more glorious than the last.

"There are sixty queens
And eighty concubines,
And virgins without number;
My dove, my perfect one,
Is the only one,
The only one of her mother,
The favorite of the one who bore her.
The daughters saw her
And called her blessed,
The queens and the concubines,
And they praised her.
Who is this she who looks forth
As the morning,
Fair as the moon,
Clear as the sun,
Awesome as an army with banners?"

Wishing to make the Shulamite feel the fervor and the exclusivity of his love, the Beloved distinguishes her from the other women. Though surrounded by 60 queens and 80 concubines and numerous other beauties, in his affections she by far is preeminent. She is his perfect one—his only one. Not only is she admired by the Beloved, she is praised by the queens, concubines, and other maidens. They show no signs of jealousy. Like a choral choir in perfect harmony, they voice their praises of her beauty. They, with the Beloved, acknowledge her beauty and call her *blessed.*

A rhetorical question (6:10)

"Who is she who looks forth as the morning, fair as the moon, clear as the sun, awesome as an army with banners?" This question seems to be posed by the daughters, the queens, and the concubines as a part of their calling her blessed and praising her. The once-obscure shepherd girl has become known and noticed by many important others. And this question is similar to the one following the minor episode in chapter three, *"Who is this coming out of the wilderness like pillars of smoke . . . ?"*

Emerging from the long dark night of separation, she rises as does the sun into a new day. She appears as the morning. "The verb in other Old Testament contexts means *to look down on something* or *the overhang.* One waits in patient expectation for the first rays of the rising sun to illuminate the gray outline of the mountain slopes. So with the girl; if the hints of her initial appearing are so enticing, what will the full manifestation reveal?"[140]

The use of the terms *"the moon"* and *"the sun"* give an impression of the supernatural influence on the girl's condition. The moon merely reflects in the night what the sun is doing during the day hours. The sun is the source of light, life, and heat. The moon on a clear dark night is a sight to behold—as awesome as the sun on a clear day, remaining a mere reflection of the sun. The Shulamite radiates a presence, as does the moon by the sun. She makes an impression on all who come within her attractive orbit.[141]

The observers pick up the Beloved's phrase *awesome as an army with banners,* from the beginning of his praise song in 6:4. His evaluation becomes the standard others use to describe the Shulamite. Through pressure, pain, and privation, enlargement occurs—not only for us but also for others. Pressure on a piece of coal produces diamonds, so pressure has produced a well-muscled young woman with strength as a mighty, victorious army. Had the Shulamite competed with these female companions, she would have minimized her influence with them.

A chariot-souled woman (6:11-12)

With the passing of seasons the garden changes. Once again the Shulamite makes custodial inspection. All at once she has her own personal epiphany.

The Shulamite:
"I went down to the garden of nuts
To see the verdure of the valley,
To see whether the vine had budded
And the pomegranates had bloomed.
Before I was even aware,
My soul had made me
As the chariots of my noble people".

She seems to be wandering alone in her garden and is deep in thought. This *"garden of nuts"* contains walnut trees. Apart from the Galilee region, Israel is too hot for the walnut; its habitat is farther north. This *garden of nuts* was an unusual one if it contains the walnut tree. The verdure of the valley is a *wadi,* a dry waterbed which only during the spring contains water. These desert areas turn a refreshing green when the early rains fall. While inspecting the plants and trees for buds and blooms, suddenly she seems to catch a glimpse of what she has become.

"My soul had made me as the chariots of my noble people." This verse is perhaps the most difficult in the Song to translate and interpret. The literal translation reads:

> *I did not know*
> *My soul (f)*
> *(She) set me*
> *Chariots (of)*
> *My people*
> *A prince*[142]

Let's connect this verse with the other garden visits (4:16 and 5:1).

(The Shulamite) *"Let my beloved come to his garden and eat its pleasant fruits."*

(The Beloved) *"I have come to my garden . . . I have gathered, I have eaten."*

(The Shulamite) *"I have come to my garden . . . ."*

She invites. Answering, he arrives, eats, and enjoys its fruit. Something happened in the interim. What is it? She has changed! Her soul was now as the chariots of her noble people.

Like a Hummer utility vehicle, a chariot is a luxury item—not owned by the average person. Belonging to *"my noble people"*, ammi-nadib means *the nobleman of my people*. To *seat with the nobles* means, in a physical sense, to raise from the ground—*to elevate someone to a higher location*. But also understand the image in terms of its symbolism: to grace an individual by the gesture of letting him sit among the power-ful.[143] This formerly poor shepherd girl not only is associated with nobility, she is nobility!

This insight is a continuation of her discovery in 6:3, *"I am my beloved's."* He has been hers all along. She is the one who holds back. Now he has total access to her life. Truly, a change has taken place—not just geographically, from a shepherd's field to a king's palace, but internally. No longer does she have an immature, dreaming, shepherd-girl's heart but a heart of nobility. She truly is Shepherd-shaped.

Married for 23 years I never think of myself by my maiden name but as Iva May. My identity as Stan's wife is much stronger than is my identity as my mother's daughter. In theory the wedding ceremony initiated the change, but actually time has transformed me. The Shulamite did not become noble-souled overnight. Though the process is lengthy, the revelation is sudden. Once again we are reminded that the Kingdom of God, unlike the Magic Kingdom, has no "fairy dust." Rather the process of growth in grace is lifelong, for God is working for and from eternity. He insists on building in grace what will take a lifetime to develop, because His goals, like His thoughts, differ so vastly from those of ours.

Mourning turned to dancing (6:13)

The Beloved and his friends:
"Return, return, O Shulamite;
Return, return,
That we may look upon you!"

The Shulamite:
"Why would you see in the Shulamite—

As it were, the dance of two camps?"

The use of the word *Shulamite* at this point in the Song is significant. This is the only time the *Shulamite* is addressed in the Song. Commenting on this address, Othmar Keel says, "*Shulamite* cannot be a regular proper name, it is a name used for its meaning or to designate a relationship."[144] *Shulamite* is the feminine form of Solomon.[145] It is the pet name for *peaceful*.[146] The word *Shulamite* means the one who is "well", "whole", or "at peace."[147] No wonder as their relationship deepens—as she comprehends what bearing his name means— she becomes whole, at peace. Truly, suffering has accomplished its purpose. She is perfected, established, strengthened and settled (1 Pet. 5:12).

Their request, "to come back", "return", or "go on, do it again and again", refers to the dance she is performing. They are saying, "Go on, dance some more!" "Encore, encore!"[148] The repetition of the word "*return*" emphasizes the urgency of their entreaty. They want to watch the Shulamite perform a dance. "*That we may look upon you*" is to see with insight and understanding, not just to "gaze on" or "look at." Here the onlookers meant to verify by examination the beauty they have had described to them.[149] This dancing is all about celebration, not seduction.

Dancing is an important part of celebration in Hebrews' lives and still is a part of the Jewish culture. In the Bible:

• King David and the people celebrated military victory with dancing.
• A dancing celebration takes place after the Egyptians drown in the Red Sea.
• The children of Israel dance as a part of celebrating the yearly feasts.

- Dancing takes place when a family member returns from battle.
- The return of the prodigal son prompts a dancing celebration.

The Hebrew word for *dance* suggests a specific dance, such as one performed by two groups or circles or rows of dancers. The phrase itself well may be the technical term for any dance characterized by two such formations.[150] One commentator identifies this particular dance as one of the dances in the wedding celebration.[151] He then suggests that the real question the Shulamite asks is, "Why do you want to look at me when there are so many others in the dance?"[152] The Song begins with the Shulamite's self-effacement induced by insecurity (1:6); now her self-effacement is born out of humility.

The word for *camp*, *mahanayim*, could mean a general military camp or a temporary tribal dwelling place. *Mahanayim* also is a place of worship and celebration; it is the place at which people meet with God. Jacob named the place where the angels of God met with him *Mahanaim*, "God's camp" (Gen. 32:1-2).

The Shulamite responds to their request with "*Why do you watch?*" "*What will you see?*" She seems to deflect any attempt to make her the center of attention. We will be the last to know and the most surprised when we reach the place of maturity. Manley Beasley used to say, "Pray that God will never let you know how spiritual you are." **Many people are destroyed by the very fact of their usefulness to God.** Their gaze turns from God to self. In turning they are undone.

I have heard the story of a Hindu man who worked with Amy Carmichael. When asked to name the holiest person he knew, He replied, "My master." When asked whether she had instructed him to say such, he replied, "In her prayers, she sees herself the most unholy woman on earth, but in her actions her holiness shines." The moment the moon moves between the sun and the world, the light is eclipsed. The moment our holiness moves between people and Jesus, we repel and darken instead of draw and reflect. True grace is always Jesus-centered.

Chapter 7

Something Old and Something New

Chapter six of the Song ends with the Shulamite's question in 6:13, *"What would you see in the Shulamite?"* Chapter seven begins by recording the Beloved's answer with a sweeping description of the Shulamite. We all have heard the expression "from head to toe," but the Beloved begins at the bottom and works his way up. In chapter four, when he speaks of her qualities, the Beloved begins with the head. In chapter five the Shulamite's description of the Beloved begins with the head as she gives a full-length summary of her Beloved. She uses plant and animal metaphors and comparisons. The Beloved compares the Shulamite with works of art and architecture made with costly materials. He is reinforcing the fact that she no longer is a common shepherd girl but rather is one of the nobility—one who is Shepherd-shaped.

From toe to head (7:1-9)

"How beautiful are your feet in sandals,
O prince's daughter!
The curves of your hips are like jewels,
The work of the hands of an artist.
Your navel is like a round goblet
Which never lacks mixed wine;
Your belly is like a heap of wheat

Fenced about with lilies.
Your two breasts are like two fawns,
Twins of a gazelle."

While our tendency is to recoil in the face of praise, the Shulamite stood, receptive of the Beloved's intimate examination. Since this is called the Song of Songs, I imagine the Beloved sings his description—a song sure to ignite her deepest passions and awaken her truest acceptance. Her recent question reveals a lingering need for affirmation. Patiently he describes to the Shulamite what he sees. She gets more than she bargains for. She seeks a word of affirmation; she receives a song of delight.

Feet
"How beautiful are your feet in sandals." The plural *pa'am* (feet) refers less typically to the feet as such (Ps. 58:11) than to their activity, "your steps."[153] The term *beautiful* refers to more than the beauty of the foot; the word identifies the acoustic effect made from the rhythmic tapping of sandals against the foot or the ground. Othmar Keel provides insight on the oriental view of the feet:

Western readers have often been surprised that sandals were thought to make feet particularly beautiful. Rural Judean women normally went barefoot. In Ezekiel 16:10, sandals were seen as decorative items. But, along with their aesthetic value, sandals have a juridical value that one dare not overlook. Sandals permit a firm step, in both the literal and figurative sense. In some situations the loosening and removal of sandals expresses a waiver of rights (Ruth 4:7; Deut. 25:5-10).[154]

Further, the word for *"feet"* also can mean a step, a pace, and interval of distance.[155] Dancing requires coordination. The Shulamite has surety of movement. African believers cannot remain stationary as they celebrate Jesus; they dance! Even though I "moved" in an awkward, uncoordinated manner, I learned to celebrate alongside the African women with whom we worshiped in Zimbabwe.

The believer is to be sure-footed as well. Paul describes the believer's walk as:

- a walk in newness of life (Rom. 6:4)
- a walk according to the Spirit (Rom. 8:1, 4)
- a walk by faith (2 Cor. 5:7)
- a walk that does not fulfill the lust of the flesh (Gal. 5:16)
- a walk of good works (Eph. 2:10)
- a worthy walk (Eph. 4:1)
- a walk in love (Eph. 5:2)
- a walk in the light (Eph. 5:8)
- a circumspect walk (Eph. 5:15)
- a walk in wisdom (Col. 4:5)
- a walk worthy of God (1 Thess. 2:12)
- a walk pleasing to God (1 Thess. 4:1)
- a proper walk toward those outside (1 Thess. 4:12)

Isaiah describes the feet of those who proclaim good news as *beautiful* (Isa. 52:7). The feet that walk according to the Word will be beautiful.

The fact that the Beloved refers to the Shulamite as the *"prince's daughter"* is fitting. *Prince* literally means one who is "liberal or generous." "The clearest sign of nobility in the OT is the opportunity and the ability to be generous."[156]

Hips

"The curves of your hips are like jewels, the work of the hands of an artist." If the feet speak of sureness of movement, then the thigh speaks of strength for movement. The curves refer to the beautiful symmetry of the lower appendage. The use of this metaphor illustrates the graceful outline and perfect beauty of the lower part of the body. She is a work of art.

The Man who wrestled with Jacob had to touch the joint of his thigh and dislocate it. Natural energy has to be crippled by God to make room for a new character who can be trusted with spiritual power. *Walk* is Paul's favorite metaphor for the Christian life. Through both intimacy and trials the Shulamite has learned to walk with the Beloved.

When the hand of the Skillful Jeweler forms the character of one of His Shulamite women, He is never clumsy or unimaginative. He has in mind a work of art that when completed will bring much attention and glory to the Artist.

Navel

"Your navel is like a round goblet which never lacks mixed wine." Some ancient Egyptian paintings emphasize the navel of the feminine form, so that some ancient cultures consider it as an object of beauty.[157] The roundness of the waist is compared to a goblet or bowl filled with spiced wine made of myrrh and fragrant cane.[158] The beauty of the waist expanding upward into the fullness of the bosom therefore is most aptly illustrated by such a goblet, to the natural beauty of which is added the beauty of the richest spiced wine.[159]

Goblets for the nobility are made of silver or gold and sometimes are inlaid with more precious metal or jewels. Several commentators write of the erotic nature of this particular feature. As the cut umbilical cord heals, it either caves in (an "innie") or out (an "outie"). Hers definitely is a cavernous "innie"—large enough to hold intoxicating wine.

Belly

"Your belly is like a heap of wheat fenced about with lilies." Not very flattering. How would you like your husband to describe your belly in such a way? This description contrasts that of the Beloved in 5:14; his body is carved ivory inlaid with sapphires. The abundance of wheat is a sign of God's blessing toward Israel. Psalm 81:16 says, *He would have fed them also with the finest of wheat; and with honey from the rock I would have satisfied you.* Lilies, too, represent abundance; they are found in abundance in the Middle East. Egyptians maintained a careful custom to decorate foodstuffs of all kinds with lotus flowers.[160] The Shulamite's physical attributes nourish and satisfy the Beloved both in appearance and in fulfillment.

Breasts

"Your two breasts are like two fawns, twins of a gazelle." The Beloved repeats what he already has said in 4:5. The soft coat of the fawn makes a person want to stroke it. The Beloved wants the Shulamite to know that her soft and gentle beauty has kindled his desire for her and that he wishes to express that desire by caressing her two breasts.

Beauty is culturally defined; Americans love small waists, while Africans prize larger women. So, what makes a woman beautiful? Believing the truth as God sees and says. What is God saying about you? His words alone hold the ring of truth; He alone defines true beauty. Do you believe Him, or are you still listening to the brassy sound made by those who trumpet physical features alone? Are you being defined by Hollywood or by the Holy One?

Head and shoulders (7:4-5)

"Your neck is like a tower of ivory,
Your eyes like the pools in Heshbon
By the gate of Bath-rabbim;
Your nose is like the tower of Lebanon,
Which faces toward Damascus.
Your head crowns you like Carmel,
And the flowing locks of your head are
*   like purple threads;*
The king is captivated by your tresses."

While her body receives the Beloved's initial interest, His attention ultimately is drawn to the Shulamite's face. The head crowns the body; the face attracts the eyes. A wisely dressed woman draws all attention to her face. Women who develop such a look cause men to look at their eyes, not at their body. Today we see why the Shulamite is head-and-shoulders above others.

The Shulamite's face is the center of His attention. She is, in a word, radiant. As she basks in his love, her face begins to radiate the joy and liberty of being loved. In 2 Corinthians 3:17-18 Paul writes of this same experience.

Neck
"Your neck is like a tower of ivory." Ivory is obtained only by sacrificial cost to the animal that produces it. The comparison to a tower suggests a strong and perhaps long neck. In Zimbabwe, as in other parts of Africa, women are trained from the ages of 3 and 4 to carry on their heads water buckets, firewood, and other items. I have seen women carry 50-pound bags of ground corn balanced on their heads as they walk along knitting and carrying a baby tied on their backs. Like an

ivory tower their necks are not developed overnight! Strong neck muscles are developed like any other muscle is—by daily use.

Ivory was treasured in ancient Israel as a rare and beautiful material—too precious for casual use. It was carved, covered with gold leaf, and inlaid with semiprecious stones. King Solomon made a great throne of ivory and overlaid it with pure gold. King Ahab built an ivory house. Not only is the neck the pedestal for the head, it is the nerve center for the rest of the body. A neck injury affects the entire body. The Beloved's compliment takes on new meaning as, using such royal metaphors, he describes her neck.

Eyes

"*Your eyes are like the pools in Heshbon by the gate of Bath-rabbim.*" In the past the Shulamite's eyes have been compared to dove's eyes. The figure of "*pools*" seems to add to the thought of depth. These reservoirs of water are known for their calm, reflective quality and are often clear and deep. A deep, clear pool invites contemplation and reflection. Perhaps the Beloved finds himself drawn to gaze into and drink from those eyes.

"*The gate of Bath-rabbim.*" *Bath Rabbim* means daughter of noble people[161] or daughter of the great and mighty. This epithet especially would be meaningful in view of the association the Song makes between Heshbon and the Shulamite, who herself is given the epithet "*nobleman's daughter*" (7:2).[162]

Heshbon was a town about 20 miles east of the point where the Jordan enters the Dead Sea; it was built for the area's abundance of pasturage, springs, and brooks from which the pools of Heshbon were supplied. "The pools of a place situated in such a country as that around Heshbon would be likely to be supplied with water purer and fresher than those of

Jerusalem."[163] They were remarkable for their purity and quietness.[164]

As he gazes into her eyes, the Beloved sees a reflection of himself. The position he has given her, the affirmation, the joy he has found in her—her eyes reflect it all. Her eyes draw him to her as the pools draw the thirsty. Reflection appears clearly on the waters that are glassy with stillness. Women today run to and fro with little time for stillness. A frantic pace dishonors the Lord and keeps the waters so stirred that the surface reveals a distorted image. Sometimes women are so busy in ministry that they neglect moments of peace and quiet. **Ministry business is often the greatest detractor to spiritual devotion.** May our eyes resemble the pools of Heshbon!

Nose

"Your nose is like the tower of Lebanon, which faces toward Damascus." The nose is an important perceptive faculty; it can distinguish what the other senses cannot. With the nose likened to the tower of Lebanon, this reference in this verse speaks of protective ability. This tower of Lebanon probably is a tower built on some part of that range of mountains in the frontiers of Israel on an elevated position overlooking the beautiful valley of Damascus. The Beloved is not saying the Shulamite has a large nose. He is describing her perceptive abilities.

Animals' noses flare and snort at the first scent of danger. Discernment grows by exercising the senses. *But solid food belongs to those who are of full age, that is, those who by reason of use have their senses exercised to discern both good and evil* (Heb. 5:14). *Discern* is from the word *diakrisis*, meaning to distinguish, to decide, to judge. A distinguishing, discerning clearly, i.e., spoken of the act or power.[165] Sometimes what is good and what is evil are not always obvious. By practice or use of the principles contained in the Word, the maturing believer will be able to distinguish between good and evil. The Shulamite has grown up; she no longer is naïve but has become wise.

Head and hair

"Your head crowns you like Carmel, And the flowing locks of your head are like purple threads; The king is captivated by your tresses." Perhaps the Beloved is describing a headdress—an accessory item. Isaiah describes some of the feminine articles of the daughter of Zion—the ornamental headdress and headbands (Isa. 3:20). Women often wore ornate headdresses; the Shulamite is no exception.

Mount Carmel is a flat-topped summit overlooking the Mediterranean Sea, where Elijah has a showdown with the prophets of Baal. On that high vantage point he sees the sign of the approaching storm (1 Kings 18:19-20; 44). From that spot he runs before Ahab to Jezreel. Carmel is about 1,400- to 1,600-feet high and was, in biblical times, fruitful, with vineyards, olive-groves, and orchards of figs and almond trees, not on the sides alone but also along the table-land of its summit.[166] Isaiah describes the future glory of Israel as a blooming desert accentuated with the glory of Lebanon and the excellence of Carmel and Sharon (Isa. 35:2).

Hair

"And the flowing locks of your head are like purple threads; the king is captivated by your tresses." *"Purple"*, another emblem of royalty, does not signal a bad hair-dye job; rather, it speaks of its luminescence:

The coastal areas beneath the majestic Mt. Carmel are the home of purple cloth. Because a single purple snail yields only a tiny amount of the coveted dye, the violet or dark-red textiles were very expensive. The comparison of the woman's hair with purple does not mean that it was "red" but that it was vital, dark, and gleaming.[167]

Her hair already has been compared to the hair of goats (4:1). Her hair again draws his attention; he is captivated by her tresses, as in a net. At the beginning of the Song, the Shulamite is held captive by her longings for romantic love. Now, he is the one held captive.

> *"How beautiful and how delightful you are,*
> *My love, with all your charms!*
> *Your stature is like a palm tree,*
> *And your breasts are like its clusters.*
> *I said, 'I will climb the palm tree,*
> *I will take hold of its fruit stalks.'*
> *Oh, may your breasts be like clusters of the vine,*
> *And the fragrance of your breath like apples,*
> *And your mouth like the best wine!"*

The palm tree

So far, we have seen the Shulamite favorably described and compared to works of art and subjects of beauty. As he continues his description, the Beloved changes his comparisons from works of art to works of nature.

The Beloved describes his overall satisfaction with the Shulamite. *"How beautiful and how delightful you are, My love, with all your charms!"* For the 10th time in the Song the Beloved erupts with endearing phrases of possession. *"My love"*, he calls her. Then using the metaphor of the palm tree he describes in the most erotic of terms his possession.

The name *Tamar* means *palm*. Several women in the Old Testament are named Tamar. For his firstborn son Judah takes a wife by this name. David's daughter, the sister to Absalom, is named Tamar and is described as *lovely* (2 Sam 13:1) and as *a woman of beautiful appearance* (2 Sam. 14:27).

In the Middle East the date palm is found in abundance. The trunk is straight and rough and grows up to 60-feet tall. At about its eighth year the palm begins yielding clusters of dates. These reach maturity at about 30 years. Each cluster of dates weighs up to 25 pounds. The annual yield of a single tree may reach up to 600 pounds.

The oriental traveler values the fruit of the date palm more than he does bread, so great is the fruit's sustaining power; the fruit-bearing powers of the tree do not pass away. As its age increases, the fruit becomes more perfect as well as more abundant. The palm also is the emblem of victory; it raises its beautiful crown toward the heavens. It is fearless of the heat of the sultry sun or of the burning hot wind from the desert.[168]

Seen from a distance this noble tree of the desert promises the traveler shelter and nourishment. Perhaps the Beloved is alluding to the Shulamite's dark complexion and notes his attraction to her because of her enduring quality of perseverance under trial. The Beloved is familiar with the trees of Lebanon; several times in the poem he mentions Lebanon. His chariot is constructed with wood from Lebanon (3:9); the scent of her garments is compared to the fragrance of Lebanon (4:11). The famous cedars of Lebanon, though tall and fragrant, do not bear delectable fruit. In order to thrive they need a colder climate. The Beloved instead chooses to compare her stature to this lovely, fruit-bearing, desert tree.

The length of the trunk draws his eyes upward to the clusters of fruit perched like birds' nests among the branches. Here we get the idea of uprightness and fruitfulness. The palm tree is an endogen. "In contrast to the exogen type of tree which derives its sustenance largely from external sources, the palm tree gets its nourishment through its deeply growing roots which tap some hidden source of supply."[169] The heart of the cedar tree is hard, while the heart of the palm tree is softer than is its exterior. Though the exterior is toughened by the heat of the sun, the heart remains soft. This enables the palm to spring back into its upright position after the beating and bending of the desert wind. It may bend, but it won't break. Though tossed by wind and storm, it refuses to grow crookedly. The fruit remains secure until maturity—ripened and waiting to be picked.

Springs of water are always found near palm trees. Jeremiah describes the man who trusts and hopes in the Lord as *a tree planted by the waters which spreads out its roots by the river, and will not fear when heat comes; but its leaf will be green, and will not be anxious in the year of drought, nor will cease from yielding fruit* (Jer. 17:7-8). During July 2003 Memphis experienced a straight-line storm with winds more than 100 miles an hour. Many Bradford pear trees were uprooted, while much larger oak trees remained standing. Bradford pear trees do not have a tap root. They toppled because they were top-heavy with little below the ground to sustain them during the storm. A healthy root system is vital.

Appropriation (7:8-9)

"I said, 'I will climb the palm tree, I will take hold of its fruit stalks.'" *"I will climb . . . I will take hold."* The Beloved expresses his intent to possess her. The Shulamite is experiencing intimacy to a capacity she could not have known earlier in their relationship. The Beloved is expressing the cost willingly paid for her delights. The rewarded sweetness is worth the climb.

Three special delights:

1. Her breasts. *"May your breasts be like clusters of the vine."* Her breasts, in the past compared to twin fawns, are compared to a cluster of fruit. This symbolizes the sweetness found there.

2. Her breath. *"and the fragrance of your breath like apples."* Her breath reflected the sweetness of what had been eaten. What is inhaled is exhaled. She spent time under the shade of his tree (2:3), ate of its fruit, and found it sweet and refreshing to her taste (2:5). Spending time with people usually gives one time to see that which fills their heart. Jesus asserts, *"Out of the abundance of the heart the mouth speaks."* As she knows his heart, she becomes dependent on his provision for her.

3. Her mouth. *"And your mouth like the best wine."* He chooses the same word the Shulamite uses in 5:16 to describe his own mouth. Her mouth or palate is sweet. Her opening wishes (1:2) now are reversed. What she desires from the Beloved (the kisses of his mouth—better than wine) he now experiences from her.

Have you ever tried, when you had a terrible cold, to detect flavor from food or a beverage? You probably tasted very little, if anything at all. Aroma receptors are situated in the back of the mouth and the throat as well as in the nose. These transmit information to the brain. The sense of smell largely determines what we taste. Pleasant aromas attract; unpleasant aromas repel. Her fragrance entices him to taste; what he tastes, he enjoys. Wine-tasters grade a wine by its color, taste, and smell. Swishing the wine in the mouth to gain full benefit of its taste is important. The Beloved gives the Shulamite perfect marks.

The end of the power struggle (7:9-10)

The Shulamite declares for the third and last time in the Song, "*I am my beloved's.*" Anxiety and fear of unrequited love finally are laid to rest. The Song begins with the Shulamite hopelessly longing for love from one so great and seemingly unattainable. She has traveled full-circle. Their desire for each other is equally matched as the Song begins its descent.

The Shulamite:
"It goes down smoothly for my beloved,
Flowing gently through the lips of those who fall asleep.
I am my beloved's,
And his desire is for me."

"Wine which tastes bad sticks in the palate but that which tastes pleasantly glides down directly and smoothly."[170] Bitter wine leaves a sour aftertaste. This wine—her love—leaves no aftertaste. Not only does it go down smoothly, its effects live on through the dreams of the satiated sleeper.

"*I am my beloved's, and his desire is toward me.*" Many say this is the high point of the Song. The Shulamite has moved from "*My beloved is mine, and I am his*" (2:16) to the sweetly satisfying experience of knowing she belongs to him, "*I am my beloved's, and my beloved is mine*" (6:3). She now has reached the apex of love—total assurance that he absolutely desires her. Her heart now knows the deepest joy and the sweetest peace. He knows her thoroughly and loves her passionately. Maturity brings security!

This phrase emphasizes mutuality. Othmar Keel suggests its emphasis on mutuality does not imply an owner's pride in the other but is like the relational formula of Genesis 2:23

(*This at last is bone of my bones and flesh of my flesh*); it expresses the feeling of deepest and most intimate connectedness. The misery of loneliness, *It is not good that the man should be alone* (Gen. 2:18), is overcome by the realization that she is there for him and he is there for her.[171] Fullness, security, peace, and freedom epitomize the relationship in which connectedness and mutual giving and receiving are experienced. **A one-sided relationship easily can degenerate into dominance and ownership.** The fact that the Shulamite expresses this thought three times in the Song demonstrates the importance of mutual desire and satisfaction.

Other than here, the word *desire* occurs only in Genesis 3:16 and 4:7, "*Your desire will be for your husband and he will rule over you*"; Sin is at the door; its desire is for you. In the Genesis context, the word has been much debated. Some have vigorously disputed the sexual element. The suggestion has been made that the woman's desire actually is to dominate her husband, as in Genesis 4:7, where sin's urge is to dominate Cain. So then the result of the fall is the disruption of mutual complement into one of a desire for mutual domination, the one over the other. Be that as it may, our lovers here in the Song are not trying to dominate each other. She is giving herself to him as his willing partner.[172]

Another commentator stated that 7:11 reads almost like a deliberate reversal of Genesis 3:16—turning it upside down by making the woman the object of desire. Instead of the domination of the man over the woman, the present verse speaks of a relationship of mutuality, expressed in a formula of reciprocal love like that in 2:16, 6:3.[173] Keels adds a further comment:

There, in connection with the curse of the serpent, the penalties announced to human beings present several of their troubles as consequences of the first sin. One of woman's troubles is that her longing for love and children produces a desire for the man, but this yearning of the female is used by the male to exercise his rule over her in an oppressive way. Here this line declares the lifting of the inequality that was the basis for such oppression. In the same way that her yearning and passion are directed toward him, his passion and yearning are now directed toward her. Thus the curse-like situation is lifted.[174]

The Shulamite discovers that her desire is eclipsed by the Beloved's desire toward her. They are the objects of each other's desire.

Oneness attained (7:11-13)

Here for the first time in the Song the Shulamite makes a direct request for the Beloved's presence. Having grown secure in his love, she feels free to initiate greater intimacy. The lovers' oneness is reflected by the phrase "*Let us.*" The prophet Amos asks, *Can two walk together unless they are agreed?* (Amos 3:3). Communion with Him means walking together with Him—united in purpose. Look at the couple's unity of purpose.

"*Come, my beloved, let us go out into the country,*
Let us spend the night in the villages.
Let us rise early and go to the vineyards;
Let us see whether the vine has budded
And its blossoms have opened,
And whether the pomegranates have bloomed.
There I will give you my love.

The mandrakes have given forth fragrance;
And over our doors are all choice fruits,
Both new and old,
Which I have saved up for you, my beloved."

The Shulamite has been preoccupied with the Beloved's house, his banqueting table, his chambers, his absences, and his admirable countenance. After times of chastisement, discipline, restoration, and intimacy with her Beloved, she seems to understand his invitations to her in the past to *"Arise up, my love, my fair one, and come away . . . in the clefts of the rocks, in the secret places of the cliff. Let me see your face. Let me hear your voice. Come with me from Lebanon my spouse, with me from Lebanon. Look from the top of Amana . . ."* Maturity awakens the ownership of responsibility. The Shulamite now seems to see beyond the immediate comfort of her surroundings and responds to the call to take responsibility for all that she shares with the Beloved.

The Shulamite answers the call to missions. The call is fourfold:

1. *"Let us go out into the country."*

The fields already have been mentioned twice in the Song (1:7; 2:7; 3:5), in which the Beloved finds rest in the fields—in the wild, among the gazelles or the does. In the fields he also finds his countrymembers—those who labor within the fields. In the fields the Shulamite urges the daughters not to stir up or awaken love until it pleases. No longer enamored with palace life she now wants to be with him in those desolate and difficult-to-work fields.

We so easily become so involved in the church that we never spend time in the place where He feeds His flocks, where He seems to be alone—in the fields. She never before had offered to join the Beloved there. Her world now has become much larger. Her actions echo the words of a song often sung at mission events, "My house is full, but my field is empty. Who will go and work for me today? It seems my children all want to sit around my table, but no one wants to work in my field."

I am reminded of my own experience when, several years ago, in my church I taught a singles Sunday-school class, a church-training class, and a weekly women's Bible study. I also taught a course as an adjunct seminary instructor for student wives. I had a small part-time job. I was busy! The Lord showed me that I was entirely too busy in the church house but uninvolved in the harvest field. I completed my commitments at church and then resigned from all three obligations (I still teach the wives' class at the seminary). I actually took a secular job and began having the time of my life meeting people whom I would never have met within the four walls of the church. For a while I missed all of the church activity but found that God's new direction allowed me to meet people and minister in a way I could not have done before.

The fact is interesting that though the disciples already had been to the city of Samaria in which the woman at the well lived, they were oblivious to the spiritual needs there. What the disciples saw as a place to purchase bread, Jesus saw as a harvest field (John 4). Some time ago I went through a period in which I stopped witnessing to people. I believed that people generally were cold and indifferent to spiritual things. God shook me loose from my unbelief as He refreshed my vision with His vision. What I saw and what He saw were radically different. He opened my eyes to the whiteness of the harvest fields; I started sharing the gospel again. Guess what? People trusted Christ! I simply needed His perspective. That the Shulamite had experienced a deeper walk with her Beloved became obvious as she embraced his world. The more intimate the communion with the Beloved, the deeper the passion for the things that captivate his attention. She became his partner in the field.

2. *"Let us spend the night in the villages."*

Lodging speaks of temporary residence, not permanency. The use of lodging and villages re-enforces this idea of pilgrimage—of sojourners passing through.

Just as the children of Israel dwelt in tents, moving when the cloud moved, so the believer never settles down this side of heaven. A willingness to remain must exist until the cloud moves and to leave when the cloud leaves. We are pilgrims and ambassadors. A pilgrim is one who roams through foreign lands. An ambassador is one who, in the place of another, represents his or her country (2 Cor. 5:20).

For more than six years we lived in Zimbabwe, Africa. By the government's invitation we lived and worked as temporary residents with temporary work permits. After six years we were invited to leave when the government chose not to extend our work visas. In the same way believers are here on earth with temporary work permits. One day they will be revoked when His work through us is complete. Many of us so pad our surroundings that leaving our comfort zone for any other place is arduous; our roots run so deep we cannot be dislodged. Just as the children of Israel had to be prepared to move when the cloud moved, we can be prepared to go with the cloud.

Neighborhoods have become status symbols instead of mission opportunities. Before, remaining in the Beloved's house and enjoying the benefits of their relationship would have been easy. The enlightened Shulamite now wants to be involved in the King's interests. Palace life no longer consumes her. The more satisfied with him and satiated by his love she is, the less enthralled she is with her palace surroundings.

3. *"Let us rise early and go to the vineyards."*

Desire drives diligence. Before, the Shulamite saw the vineyards as a burden—as work (1:6). Now she is quite eager to go forth to his vineyards; "Let us get up early," she says. This indicates her diligence and urgency. Desire drives diligence. A person really does exactly what he or she wants to do. The difference between industriousness of a spiritual character and spiritual slothfulness lies in the use of time.[175] The book of Proverbs has much to say to the sluggard—the one lacking in this virtue of diligence.

- Poverty happens to the one who uses sleep to get out of work (Prov. 6:9-11).
- The lazy man will become a slave (Prov. 12:24).
- The slothful man is no different than a great destroyer (Prov. 18:9).
- The lazy person will go hungry (Prov. 19:15, 24).
- The lazy person will become a beggar (Prov. 20:4).

The Proverbs 31 woman exemplifies this virtue of diligence. She is too busy to stay in bed. She rises early to provide food for her household; she retires at night only when the work is done.

Not only is the Shulamite early at work, she is at work with him. She has discovered that a place of labor with the Beloved is more to be desired than is ease without him. No longer does she mind having her feet dirty. Before, the field is undesirable—a place of drudgery to be escaped by daydreaming. No longer alone in the work of the vineyard, the

Shulamite enjoys the work. Ruth Stewart says that so much of the trouble in church work today arises "because saints go into the vineyard without Him; the hatreds, the misunderstanding, and the terrible lack of love in the fellowship"[176] give evidence to this independent spirit. Jesus, however, categorically says no genuine and lasting fruit occurs unless one abides in Him (John 15:4-5). When ministry becomes burdensome, it is a good indicator that we are trying to work the vineyards alone without Him.

4. *"Let us see whether the vine budded."*

You investigate the things in which you invest. Sometime ago Stan and I invested in a small mutual fund. Before we made this investment, I had never paid attention to the stock market. Now, I am highly motivated to track the market to keep an eye on my investment. I have another investment as well. Every year we give sacrificially to missions. I eagerly read the missions magazine of our denomination and pray for our missionaries. Because I am heavily invested in missions, I keep watch over my investment in the proclamation of the gospel to the peoples of the world. The Shulamite had an investment in the vineyard; she kept abreast of its progress. She looks to see whether the grape blossoms are open and the pomegranates are in bloom. There she gives him her love.

Fruitfulness is the Shulamite's main emphasis at this point in their relationship. She wants results. Before, work is a distraction. Now that she has entered into a place of mature union, the fruit of her union is evident by her interest in the work of the fields. Many who name the name of Jesus are virtually uninterested in bearing a spiritually fruitful life.

"The mandrakes have given forth fragrance." The mandrake is a love plant and, as in Genesis 30:14-16, signifies the most intimate union between husband and wife.[177] In *The*

Zondervan Pictorial Bible Dictionary, John L. Leedy further defines the mandrake:

> A member of the potato family, the mandrake is also called "love-apple." The "apples", although insipid-tasting and slightly poisonous, are much desired as edible fruit. The mandrake root is large, sometimes resembling the human body in shape. It was used as a charm against the evil spirits and, as indicated by the story of Rachael and Leah, was credited with aphrodisiac qualities.[178]

The husband of the virtuous woman in Proverbs 31 is known at the gates among his peers (Prov. 31:23). Her industriousness makes him great—makes him famous and highly esteemed among the elders ruling at the gates. Jesus expresses His desire for the believer's fruitfulness because of the glory and fame it brings to the Father and the evidence it gives of an intimate relationship with Him (John 15:8).

"And over our doors are all choice fruits, both new and old." This reminds me of wedding preparation in which the bride wears something old—perhaps an heirloom necklace or other piece of jewelry—and something new.

Things old

With joy and thanksgiving the Shulamite remembers the first things, when she was a poor shepherd girl, darkened by the desert sun—when she was lonely, seeking love and finding none. She remembers how the Beloved entered her life, filled it with gladness and joy, and lavished on her his great love and wealth. Her careless heart had caused her to stray from him, to sleep when he needed her, and to resist further advances. His seeking after her, restoring her in his favor, and exalting her before their friends causes her to marvel at such great love. She brings her selflessness and her interest in his endeavors to the gates as an exhibit magnifying the depth of their union.

Things new

Relationships often become static and boring as they settle for the status quo. Room for growth always exists. Relationships never arrive; they just keep on maturing. Have you settled down and quit growing in your marriage or in your relationship with the Heavenly Beloved? Yesterday's experiences are like ashes left over from yesterday's fire. **Ashes don't bring enjoyment; only fires do.** Out go the flames of the fire unless rekindled. Though the flames in chapter five hit an all-time low, she was quick to arise and rekindle this flame.

Chapter 8

Mature Love

The Shulamite has experienced tremendous personal growth. When we began this study, we find her a needy young girl; as we conclude this study, we see a tremendously fulfilled woman. Love has transformed her. Others who have watched her progress are amazed by this transformation. No longer held back by her own shortcomings and marital misconceptions, the Shulamite is unrestrained as she expresses her desire for the Beloved's affections.

In the spotlight (8:1-5, 8-9, 13)

"Oh, that you were like a brother to me
Who nursed at my mother's breasts.
If I found you outdoors, I would kiss you;
No one would despise me, either."

"Oh, that you were like a brother to me who who nursed at my mother's breasts." If the Beloved were her brother, she could display her affection freely in public without being exposed to contempt or reprimand or even being mistaken for a harlot. The Shulamite's desire does not imply that she wishes for a brother-sister relation with the Beloved. A brother is someone to whom she could show her affection legitimately in public. What is permissible for siblings in public is in poor

taste for lovers. Holding hands testifies of a bond between individuals. Hands clasped together speak of camaraderie.

In Africa men holding hands with men and women with women is a common sight—a display of brotherhood. As an African converses with a Westerner, he or she sometimes holds the hand of a counterpart until it the hand is sweaty and uncomfortable. The Shulamite simply wants a public link to her Beloved. A love so great is not to be lived out in secrecy.

Shared experiences bond people together. Just as siblings share at their mother's breast, so, too, the lovers share experiences. Only in Western society does a mother hide while she nurses her infant. We had not been in Africa long when I saw my husband pause embarrassingly during a sermon delivery. I looked around to the spot his eyes obviously were avoiding. A young woman with fully exposed breasts was nursing her baby right there in the worship service! When I nursed my children, I sought privacy by hiding them beneath a blanket. This very natural and nurturing act of breastfeeding has been looked on by many in the West as almost shameful. The Shulamite simply desires a similar opportunity for openness to display affection toward her beloved.

> *"If I found you outdoors, I would kiss you; no one*
> *would despise me, either.*
> *I would lead you and bring you*
> *Into the house of my mother, who used to instruct me;*
> *I would give you spiced wine to drink from the juice of*
> *my pomegranates."*

"I would bring you . . . into the house of my mother." For the second time in the Song the Shulamite brings the Beloved to the house of her mother (3:4). Conflict often arises between teen-age daughters and their mothers. Adulthood is the threshold over which mothers and daughters cross into a new arena where they learn to relate as two women—as moms and friends. Moms are challenged to back off being "mommy"; (You will always be the mother, but cease the mothering when the young person becomes an adult!) daughters step forward to become friends.

Just last week my soon-to-be 22-year-old daughter reminisced a childhood experience with the words, "When I was a kid . . .." I looked at her and had an epiphany: *Jennifer is my adult daughter.* With that realization spring respect, admiration, and change. Unsolicited instruction no longer is required. With adult children that is called *meddling*!

Marriage is another threshold changing the dynamics of the mother and daughter relationship. On the handle of this door hangs a "do-not-disturb"sign. Resentment and unnecessary conflict will result if the mom ignores this door hanger and crosses that threshold. The mother, though, can place an attractive welcome mat at her own door. When her daughter is ready, she will arrive.

"*I would give you spiced wine to drink from the juice of my pomegranates.*" Wine is a frequent picture in the Song, but this is the only reference to "*spiced*" wine. Perhaps the Shulamite is demonstrating her maturity as she offers herself for the Beloved's intoxication and satisfaction. **True devotion seeks to give rather than to receive;** the needs of others are more important than are our own. Enthusiastically she finds satisfaction in his satisfaction. His pleasure is her pleasure.

Look who's watching

This chapter identifies four groups of observers: the mother, the daughters of Jerusalem, the Beloved, and her brothers.

1. The mother (8:1-2)

"My mother, who used to instruct me." The success and reward for instructing the Shulamite in the "facts of life" are seen by the Shulamite's return visit to the home of her mother. Her success is her mother's success.

A healthy marriage communicates to the children a healthy understanding of the place of intimacy within the marriage. I grew up with no knowledge that my parents had a sexual relationship; outside the bedroom they showed absolutely no affection to each other. In fact our home was fairly shorn of any physical affection. I hope that from observing our marriage our kids have a healthier view of marital intimacy.

Many mothers communicate to their daughters a negative attitude about sex, as if sex is to be avoided as often as possible except for having children and avoided totally after the childbearing years. Mothers and other female mentors have an obligation toward their daughters in this area. A few weeks before my marriage a mentor told me that sex was messy and something only to endure but not enjoy. Another mentor gave me negative instruction about sex. That negative impression tainted our first years of marriage. The Shulamite rejoiced in what she had learned from her mother—what she had integrated into her own marriage and wanted to show off!

Naomi was Ruth's mother-in-law. After her son died Naomi instructed Ruth in the art of Jewish courtship.

She told her to

> *"wash yourself and anoint yourself, put on your best garment and go down to the threshing floor; but do not make yourself known to the man until he has finished eating and drinking. Then it shall be, when he lies down, that you shall notice the place where he lies;*

and you shall go in and uncover his feet, and lie down;
and he will tell you what you should do" (Ruth 3:2-3).

Though what she instructs Ruth to do seems seductive or
flirtatious, it is not. Many young women, because of their
mothers' broken marriages and lack of mentoring, have been
robbed of needed instruction and modeling.

Not only has the Christian family and home been battered
by our divorce-driven culture, the church, too, has experienced
a real breakdown. Paul exhorted the older women to maintain
a reverent lifestyle and to teach the young women to love their
husbands, to love their children, to be discreet, homemakers,
good, and obedient to their own husbands, that the word of
God may not be blasphemed (Titus 2:4-5). To the detriment of
Christian homes our churches' older women are retiring and
leaving the younger women to counsel the younger women.

2. The daughters (8:3-4)

(To the daughters of Jerusalem):
"Let his left hand be under my head,
And his right hand embrace me."
"I want you to swear, O daughters of Jerusalem,
Do not arouse or awaken my love until she pleases."

This is the third and final time in the Song that the
Shulamite charges the daughters of Jerusalem to protect the
lovers' intimacy and the second time she refers to his left and
right hand embracing her head and heart (2:6-7). Those nearest
us may think we are impractical or too fanatical in our expression of devotion to our Beloved and will seek to interrupt our
love. Daily demands and difficult children often distract our

devotion (the house has to be cleaned, the children tended to, etc.). Our relationship with the Beloved has to be protected even from the necessary duties of life. Often the busiest and most burdened young mothers are the most guilty of neglecting their devotional lives.

3. The Beloved (8:5)
A Relative:
"Who is this coming up from the wilderness,
Leaning on her beloved?"

Some controversy exists in identifying the one asking this question. The NKJV attributes the question to an unnamed relative. However the question appears to be a rhetorical one. The observation is of great importance. Clearly all those observing this love relationship approved of what they saw—one who leans on her beloved. Earlier the Shulamite emerged from the wilderness like a pillar of smoke—heavily perfumed from her experience (3:6). Here she appears proudly dependent—leaning on her beloved. The wilderness experience has a way of leaving its mark on an individual.

The mark of maturity in child-rearing is independence. The older the child becomes, the less he or she depends on the parent. Not so in the life of the Shulamite, not with marriage, or with the believer. In fact that is the problem with so many modern marriages: partners often live independently of each other (separate bank accounts, etc.). Observing godly older couples, one can tell that they not only are deeply dependent but also are intensely protective of one another. Their lives are very much intertwined. Dependence on the Beloved by the Shulamite characterizes her maturity in the same way spiritual maturity requires the believer to rely utterly on the Lord.

I enjoy watching the interaction between Dr. B. Gray Allison (president emeritus, Mid-America Baptist Theological Seminary) and his wife, Voncille; they both are in their 80s and have been married 60-plus years. With arms interlocking they walk together as she leans on him for support. The clinging hand and the leaning posture of the Shulamite are a testimony of the strength and capability of the Beloved.

Oh, how we need the trials of the wilderness to break our will and expose our independence! Only then will we experience His Strength and His Authority as a Beloved King. Just as the husband of the Proverbs 31 woman is known in the gates, so, too, will the Heavenly Beloved be known in the gates as the one who is dependable, able to provide for, and protect, nurture, and support. He is what women really want.

"Beneath the apple tree I awakened you;
There your mother was in labor with you,
There she was in labor and gave you birth."

The Beloved is reminded of an earlier intimate moment shared under the apple tree (2:3). Recalling former days of youthful passion and expressing gratitude for what your pleasure cost another is important.

Love is jealous (8:6-7)

Many people seem content to live in the fantasy world of make-believe and mistake desire for attainment. We know much better what having spiritual desires after Christ involves than we know what reaching experientially their full satisfaction involves.[182] Not so with the Shulamite. Her longings are completely and satisfactorily fulfilled. Just as every girder in a bridge is tested, not in the hope it will break but to prove it can take the strain, so, too, has the love of the Shulamite been tested and found to be well-grounded. J. I. Packer defines jealousy as a "praiseworthy zeal to preserve something supremely precious"[183] and "as the fruit of marital affection" which results in a "zeal to protect a love-relationship, or to avenge it when broken." Like an over-zealous lover, the Shulamite jealously guards their love.

The Shulamite to her beloved:
"Put me like a seal over your heart,
Like a seal on your arm.
For love is as strong as death,
Jealousy as severe as Sheol;
Its flashes are flashes of fire,
The very flame of the Lord.
Many waters cannot quench love,
Nor will rivers overflow it;
If a man would give all the riches of his house for love,
It would be utterly despised."

The seal
"Put me like a seal over your heart, like a seal on your arm." In this verse the Hebrew word *am* means "a hand."[184] The seal refers to a signet ring; a seal serves as a form of identification. A man must never be parted from his seal. It was his automatic signature, by which important obligations could be authorized.[185] As a signet ring leaves its image/impression on the wax, so the Shulamite seeks the Beloved's imprint/impression on her life and hers on His life.

Having possession of another's seal of identification is equivalent to having free access to all his or her possessions. The Shulamite's request is mirrored by Queen Esther's receiving of Ahasuerus's signet ring, "You yourselves write a decree concerning the Jews, as you please, in the king's name, and seal it with the king's signet ring; for whatever is written in the king's name and sealed with the king's signet ring no one can revoke" (Esth. 8:8). In this manner his full authority is transferred to Esther. It has the same power as though the king himself makes the decree. The Shulamite asks that she be his identifying mark.

Jesus is God's identification of Himself to the world. When Phillip asked Jesus to reveal the Father, Jesus said, *"He who has seen Me has seen the Father"* (John 14:9). Jesus describes the believer as *"being sealed with the Holy Spirit of promise"* (Eph. 1:13). The Holy Spirit is the legal mark of ownership. He leaves God's impression on the wax of our lives.

Love and jealousy

Love and jealousy are corresponding emotions. Jealousy is a byproduct of love. The more ardent the love, the more intense the jealousy.

Love is as strong as death

"For love is as strong as death." No one escapes death. It is sure and inevitable. The death of Christ on the cross is the proof of God's love for sinners. One only has to look at the cross to know that God is love. Love's intensity blazes forth from the cross and the tomb. The strength of God's love for others is seen by Christ's death. The proof of God's love is seen in Christ's resurrection.

Love is impossible to quench or drown

"Many waters cannot quench love, nor will rivers overflow it." The power of anything must be determined by looking at the resistance which it may be able to overcome.[186] Love con-

tains power and force; barriers and boundaries are nothing in love's pathway. Storm's devastations are often reported on the news; entire towns are destroyed by much rain, hail, and powerful winds. Nothing can stand in the way of a tornado or hurricane. The excellence of a vessel—the power of its machinery—is shown by the angry tempests amidst which it can live and the stormy waves through which it urges its way.[187] John Shedd once said, "A ship in harbor is safe, but that is not what ships are made for." Thrust out into the sea of difficulty, the Shulamite's love could not be destroyed. In fact her love was strengthened on the waves of the sea tossed by the wind.

The criminal activity of the thief crucified on the cross next to Jesus was no barrier to His love. The foolishness of the prodigal son did not diminish the father's love for his son. A woman's immorality, a man's demon-possession, a man's shortness of stature, or even the shame of the publican did not hinder the outflow of love from Jesus. Neither immaturity nor neglect nor defiance nor stubbornness could lessen the love that the Beloved had for the Shulamite. Paul records a list of barriers that cannot interfere with God's love for the believer: tribulation, distress, persecution, famine, nakedness, peril, or sword (Rom. 8:38-39).

Incomparable to wealth

Perhaps the most memorable story of the 20th century recounts the love of King Edward VIII of England, who abdicated his throne for the American commoner Wallis Warfield Simpson. One of love's chief attributes is its single-minded passion that pays the purchase price. In telling the parable of the hidden treasure, Jesus says, *"For the joy over it [the treasure hidden in the field], he goes and sells all that he has and buys that field"* (Matt. 13:44). The worth of an item is demonstrated by the price paid.

Jealousy is cruel as the grave

Jealousy is as cruel as the grave. No place is as cruel and unyielding as the grave is to the young mother burying her newborn child. To the grieving widow married for 40 years, the closed casket represents the end of soul companionship. The man interring the mother of his young children faces the harsh reality of the cold, dark dirt and its inability to return life. This passage affirms that in godly love a righteous jealousy is as hard and as inevitable as the grave. Betrayed love evokes strong passion.

Jealousy is as flames of fire

Its flames are flames of fire—a most vehement flame. Literally "its sparks are sparks of fire, an enormous flame."[188] A spark, though minute in size, carries great potential. Forest fires generally do not begin because of large fires but instead because of casual or accidental sparks. The Song's lovers' flame, which began with a small spark of mutual interest, grew into a monumental fire that several thousand years later burns brightly to readers.

How the fire burns is in accordance to the material which it consumes. It has both positive and negative effects. The same fire that melts wax hardens or bakes clay. The same fire that purifies gold makes ashes of wood.

Fire's positive effect
Fire protects and purifies.
- The Angel of the Lord appeared to Moses in the flame of fire from the midst of a bush. The miracle is not so much the burning bush but the fuelless fire. God needs nothing outside of Himself to burn! He is self-contained (Ex. 3:2) and totally consuming (Heb. 12:29).

- The cloud of the Lord hovered over the temple of the Lord during the day, and fire crowned it by night. The cloud and the fire could be seen for miles around and was a testimony of God's watchcare (Ex. 40:38).
- The Lord was a consuming fire that went before the children of Israel to destroy and dispossess their enemies (Deut. 9:3).
- When Elisha prayed and asked the Lord to open the eyes of his servant, the young man saw that the mountains were full of horses and chariots of fire all around (2 Kings 6:17).
- The purity of God's Word is likened to silver, which seven times has been refined by fire (Ps. 12:6).
- Just as precious metals are refined in the furnace, so, too, is the heart of humankind refined in the furnace's fire (Prov. 17:3).
- God promised Jerusalem that it would not need walls of stone because He would be a wall of fire around it (Zech. 2:5).
- The refiner's fire purifies precious metal, so the Lord Himself purifies His people (Mal. 3:2).
- The genuineness of one's faith is proved in the fire (1 Pet. 1:7).

Fire's negative effect

Through total consumption fire tries what is bad and leaves nothing but ashes. Note the following negative functions of fire:

- When the people complained against the Lord, the fire of the Lord consumed them (Num. 11:1-3).
- Two groups sent by the king to capture Elijah were destroyed by fire at Elijah's word (1 Kings 1:12).

- Fire one day will devour sinners and hypocrites, but the righteous will be unafraid (Isa. 33:14).
- Every Christian's work will be tested by fire and will be revealed for eternal worth (1 Cor. 3:13).
- The vengeance of eternal fire will be experienced by those given over to sexual immorality (Jude 7).
- Everyone not listed in the Book of Life will be cast into the lake of fire (Rev. 20:15).

The residents of the Northwestern states dread long, dry summers. Raging forest fires are difficult to contain and destroy thousands of acres of our national forests every summer. Several years ago while we visited the Northwest, we toured the reforested areas of Oregon which five years ago were ravaged by fire. Even today effects of past fires are evidenced.

God is a consuming fire.

This is the only time in the Song that the Lord is mentioned. Love flashes fire, *"the very flame of the Lord"* (verse 6). The NKJV translates this reference to the Lord as "a most vehement flame." In Deuteronomy 4:24 God is described as a consuming fire and a jealous God. I have met Christians who believe that the God of the Old Testament differs from the God of the New Testament. Not so. The same words in the Old Testament, *consuming fire*, are used to describe God in the New Testament (Heb. 12:29). As a consuming fire God offers the children of Israel:
- a purity in which they might dwell unharmed
- a jealousy which would tolerate no rival
- an anger which would confront sin
- a power that will guard its own because of ownership love.[189]

He is righteously and rightfully jealous. A man who would proclaim his love for his wife and not be jealous for her honor acts unworthily of love. God would be unworthy to proclaim His love for believers if He did not demand first place in our hearts. Recipient of such passion and sacrificial love, the Shulamite woman responds with zeal and fervor. She has become "a woman of one thing."

4. The brothers (8:8-9)

Earlier in the Song the Shulamite's brothers are angry with her and treat her harshly, *"My mother's sons were angry with me; they made me the keeper of the vineyard"* (1:6). Now they express an altogether new opinion of their sister.

The Shulamite's brothers:
We have a little sister and she has no breasts;
What shall we do for our sister
On the day when she is spoken for?
If she is a wall,
We shall build upon her a battlement of silver;
But if she is a door,
We shall barricade her with planks of cedar.

In the Bible brothers often take responsibility for their sisters. The story of Dinah depicts graphically the strong oriental care siblings expressed for their sisters. Levi and Simeon acted on Dinah's behalf after she was violated by Shechem, the son of Hamor. They tricked the men from Shechem's village into being circumcised. During their pain and recovery time the brothers killed them and plundered all of their possessions. In their explanation to their father for their behavior they said, *"Should he treat our sister as a harlot?"* (Gen. 34:31, NKJV).

Tamar, the daughter of King David, provides another clear example of a brother's taking responsibility to protect a sister's honor. Tamar is raped by her half-brother, Amnon, and then discarded at his whim. Distraught, ripping her clothing, and covering herself with ashes, she has nowhere to take her shame. Desolate, she spends the remainder of her life living under the roof and protection of Absalom, her oldest brother. Though he spent two years formulating his plan, Absalom had Amnon killed (2 Samuel 13 contains the story in its entirety).

A further example is found in the 21st chapter of the book of Judges. At the yearly feast of the Lord in Shiloh the daughters of Shiloh emerge to perform a dance. To provide wives to perpetuate the depleted tribe of Benjamin, the men of Benjamin capture the young dancers. Their fathers and brothers rightly complain about their abduction.

Earlier in the Song the brothers overwork the Shulamite and appear to have little concern for her welfare. Now that she is married to a king, they are quite interested in her well-being. They now have a vested interest. Who would not want the king as a brother-in-law?

Among the AmaNdebele tribe in Zimbabwe, Africa, a married man calls his wife's brother "father-in-law", because with the father they share responsibility for the sister. The brothers' relationship with the Shulamite is similar. Their paternalistic and condescending attitude re-surfaces in the Song. The Shulamite's response reflects a heart of forgiveness toward them. Their treatment, seeming harsh at the time, kept her busy and protected her chastity. They acted out of a desire to protect the family honor and guard her purity until the time of her marriage. As Patterson said, "Promiscuity might bring reproach on the family and hinder her opportunity to have a wholesome life of her own."[179] Genuine yet unconstrained longings can lead to trouble; manual labor, forced by her brothers, prohibits finding an unrighteous outlet for legitimate longings.

The brothers employ the two pictures of a wall or a door to describe their sister's purity. *"If she is a wall, we shall build on her a battlement of silver; but if she is a door, we shall barricade her with planks of cedar."* Robert Gordis acknowledges, "The passage is usually taken to express a contrast between the alternatives of the chastity of the maiden (*"if she is a wall"*) and her looseness (*"if she is a door"*)."[180] Patterson amplifies this difference by saying, "wall is impregnable and therefore represents moral resistance to sexual temptation, whereas a door may be opened or closed at will and hence represents moral weakness."[181] Having guarded her earlier on they are rewarded by her purity saved for this Beloved King.

No longer does she resent the difficult work imposed on her by her brothers. She now recognizes that their boundaries actually prevent her from becoming an open door to every testosterone-driven male and make her a wall—saved for her lover alone. In the end the Shulamite is blessed by her brothers. The providence of God, seen through those He has placed in our lives to shield and protect, heightens the past and illuminates the present. We can rejoice because He has been working all along and we did not know it.

Genesis 34 records another story about a sister and her brothers. Perhaps, not having enough to do, Dinah has too much time on her hands, so she wanders around and gains the attention of Shechem, the son of Hamor the Hivite, who takes advantage of her. Placed in a face-saving situation, Dinah's brothers avenge her honor by deceiving and murdering Shechem and his family. Brothers are protectors.

Affirmation is obtained from the Shulamite's family, her friends, and other observers. Though nice to have it doesn't change the nature of what the lovers share. Approval of others is like the tail of the pig—though flattering, it doesn't change the taste of the pork. The observations of others pale in comparison to the affirmation given by the Beloved.

A healthy tension exists between our private and public lives. Something, however, is spiritually wholesome about the one who equally conveys both privately and publicly the affection he or she has for the Beloved. Feeling stifled many are attracted to the non-traditional worship service because of the freedom to display affection publicly (raising of hands, etc.). The idea that others may demean us often restrains our own public display of affection for our Beloved.

King David reproves Michal, his wife, in her attempt to manipulate his public display of worship (2 Sam. 6:12-23) by holding him in contempt. How often do we withhold an outward display of affection for Christ around nominal believers and unbelievers because we fear their disapproval?

After the September 11 World Trade Center bombing, I watched Anne Graham Lotz speak with a commentator on Fox News. I was refreshed by her boldness about the gospel and about the exclusivity of our Lord Jesus Christ. So often we back down as we bow to political correctness and the overemphasized tolerance totem. The Shulamite does not allow even those closest to her to interfere with what she has paid such a dear price to obtain.

The Wow Factor! (8:10)

The Shulamite:
"I was a wall, and my breasts were like towers;
Then I became in his eyes as one who finds peace."

The Song begins with the Shulamite's adolescent vulnerability and romantic immaturity—when she is naïve and young. It concludes with the Shulamite's strength and confidence as a mature woman. *"I was a wall."* She assesses herself realistically.

"And my breasts were like towers." The Beloved compares her breasts to twin fawns. She, from another perspective, describes her breasts differently—as towers. A fire tower stands elevated above the forest it seeks to protect. Men and women see breasts differently. Men are stimulated sexually by the sight of a woman's breasts. For women breasts are more functional than sexual. *As a loving deer and a graceful doe, let her* [your own wife's] *breasts satisfy you at all times; and always be enraptured with her love* (Prov. 5:19). A man's only righteous sexual outlet is his own wife. Like the Shulamite a wise woman sees her breasts as towers—the place in which her husband is satisfied and protected from adultery.

"As one who finds peace." *Peace* or *shalom* can be translated as *completeness*, *harmony*, or *wholeness*.The central concept of the Hebrew term is one of unimpeded relationships with others and fulfillment in one's own undertakings. This word clearly references the Shulamite as the *completed one* of 6:13.[190] Personal fulfillment is found as she gives her life, her love, and her body to her husband. Only by their union is she made complete.

Heart attitudes eventually surface. I've already mentioned the quote, "You become on the outside what you are on the inside." The Shulamite transforms into a mature woman as she believes and integrates the Beloved's truth about her. The radiance on the inside cannot help but seep through the pores of her soul.

The Midas touch (8:11)

Everything Solomon touches prospers. His extensive properties, which he leases to vineyard keepers, are prosperous to owner and tenant alike. *"Baal-hamon"* means *owner of great wealth*.[191] He is detached from his vineyards and merely sees them as a source of revenue.[192] He has others do all the work in his vineyards and yet makes five times the profit of those who actually do the labor.[193] The point seems to be the comparison between the two vineyards. He has always had the resources at hand to develop his property. She has not.

> *"Solomon had a vineyard at Baal-hamon;*
> *He entrusted the vineyard to caretakers;*
> *Each one was to bring a thousand shekels of silver*
> *   for its fruit."*

(To Solomon):
> *"My very own vineyard is at my disposal;*
> *The thousand shekels are for you, Solomon,*
> *And two hundred are for those who take care of its*
> *   fruit."*

The untended vineyard of 1:6 now has become productive. The Beloved's vineyard yields a different return from that which is produced by the Shulamite's vineyard. His vineyards reward him monetarily; the Shulamite's vineyards reward him with sensual delights and everlasting love. His love for her has given her the freedom and ability to develop her own vineyards. In comparison to what he has gained from his vineyards, hers (now tended and flourishing) produces a superior product. Fruitfulness is the goal of a vineyard. One only has to read the creation account in Genesis to see that God's goal is fruitfulness. After He created the earth, *He commanded that it bring forth grass, the herb that yields seed and the fruit tree that yields fruit according to its kind, whose seed is in it, on the earth* (Gen. 1:11).

And they lived happily ever after (8:13-14)

Everyone loves a happy ending. As we arrive at the end of this study on the Song of Songs, we, too, can rejoice. The Shulamite has not only encountered and experienced true love; she has discovered herself.

The Beloved:
"O you who sit in the gardens,
My companions are listening for your voice—
Let me hear it!"

She dwells in the gardens. The Shulamite is in her element. She dwells in the midst of productivity. Surrounded by the fruit of her toil she is immensely happy.

"My companions are listening for your voice." The Shulamite has presence; wherever she goes, people notice. When she speaks, people listen. She influences everyone she meets. Her trials have produced in her a life-message—a message for which others yearn.

No greater joy exists than that which is found in the heart of the one who gave birth to this song she sings. He, the Beloved, invites her song—her melody of contentment and love. He relishes in her triumphant soul overflowing with joy and song. *"Let me hear it!"* Knowing that he is the cause for her song, the Beloved expresses the pride he feels as he watches this queen-bride of his sing.

Love's happy ending (verse 14)

The Shulamite:
"Hurry, my beloved,
And be like a gazelle or a young stag
On the mountains of spices."

"I am here and I am yours. Arrive when you please, but please hurry. No hesitations, no requirements, and no reservations, just arrive"—a life of open access. She has journeyed a long way. Before (2:8), the Beloved leaped on the mountains and skipped on the hills like a gazelle or young stag standing behind the wall, looking through the windows, and gazing through the lattice. Now no wall between them exists; no windows or lattice offer barriers or create distance. He has easy access to her life.

The Song begins with the Beloved bringing the Shulamite from the fields and vineyards into his banqueting house and chamber and out into his fields. He unfurls his banner of love over her that all might see that she has found favor in his sight. And they lived happily ever after.

The end.

Bibliography

Archer, Gleason, R., Laird Harris, and Bruce Waltke. *Theological Wordbook of the Old Testament.* 2 Vol. Chicago: Moody, 1980.

Bloch, Ariel, and Chana Bloch. *The Song of Songs.* New York: Random House, 1995.

Boa, Kenneth. *That I May Know Him.* Sisters, OR: Multnomah Press, 1998.

Brand, Paul. *In His Image.* Grand Rapids, MI: Zondervan, 1984.

Burrows, George. *A Commentary on the Song of Solomon.* Edinburgh, Scotland: The Banner of Truth Trust, 1853.

Carmichael, Amy. *God harden me . . .* The Dohnavur Fellowship, n.d.

Carr, G. Lloyd. *Song of Solomon.* Downers Grove, IL: IVP, 1984.

Coates, C. A. *An Outline of the Song of Songs.* Great Britain: Purnell & Sons, n.d.

Cole, R.A. *The New Bible Dictionary.* Grand Rapids: Eerdmans, 1962.

Crabb, Larry. *Finding God.* Grand Rapids: Zondervan, 1993.

_____. *Shattered Dreams.* Colorado Springs, CO: Waterbrook Press, 2001.

_____. *Understanding People.* Grand Rapids: Zondervan, 1987.

Delitzsch, F[ranz]. *Proverbs, Ecclesiastes, Song of Solomon. Vol. 6, Commentary on the Old Testament: In Ten Volumes.* C. F. Keil and F. Delitzsch. Translated by James Martin. Grand Rapids: Eerdmans, 1978 rep.

Dunn, Ron. *When Heaven Is Silent.* Nashville: Thomas Nelson, 1994.

Garrett, Duane A. *Proverbs, Ecclesiastes, Song of Solomon. The New American Commentary, Vol. 14.* Nashville: Broadman, 1993.

Gledhill, Tom. *The Message of the Song of Songs.* Downers Grove, IL: InterVarsity Press, 1994.

Gordis, Robert. *The Song of Songs and Lamentations: A Study, Modern Translation, and Commentary.* New York, KTAV, 1954.

Goulder, Michael D. *The Song of Fourteen Songs. Journal for the Study of the Old Testament. Supplement Series 36.* Great Britain: Redwood Burn, 1986.

Ironside, H. A. *Addresses on the Song of Solomon.* New York: L.B. Printing, 1933.

Jamison, Kay Redfield. "Out of Character: A Reader's Digest Face to Face Interview with Sally Field." *Reader's Digest* (May 2001): 88-95.

Jensen, Irving L. *Jensen's Survey of the Old Testament.* Chicago: Moody, 1978.

Keel, Othmar. *The Song of Songs.* Minneapolis: Fortress, 1994.

Lambert, D. W. *Oswald Chambers: An Unbribed Soul.* Fort Washington, PA: Christian Literature Crusade, 1983.

Loveless, Wendell P. *Christ and the Believer in the Song of Songs.* Chicago: Moody Bible Institute, 1945.

M. M. B. *The Song of Songs.* Pittsburgh, PA: Bethany House, 1944.

MacArthur, John. *The Glory of Heaven: The Truth about Heaven, Angels, and Eternal Life.* Wheaton, IL: Crossway, 1998.

Mack, Clinton. "Animals of the Bible", *The Zondervan Pictorial Bible*

Dictionary. Merrill C. Tenney, gen. ed. Grand Rapids: Zondervan, Regency, 1963.

McGee, Robert S. *Search For Significance.* Nashville: LifeWay Press, 1992.

McPhee, L[ouise] M. *The Romance of the Ages.* Oak Park, IL: Designed Products, 1950.

Merriam Webster's Collegiate Dictionary. 10th ed. Springfield, MA: Merriam-Webster, 1994.

Miller, Andrew. *Meditations on the Song of Solomon.* London: Walter G. Wheeler, n.d.

Nee, Watchman. *Song of Songs.* Fort Washington, PA: Christian Literature Crusade, 1965.

Patterson, Paige. *Song of Solomon.* Chicago: Moody, 1986.

Piper, John. *The Hidden Smile of God.* Wheaton IL: Crossway Books, 2001.

_____. *A Godward Life.* Sisters, OR: Multnomah, 1997.

Stewart, Ruth. *Better than Wine.* Asheville, NC: Revival Literature, 1970.

Strong, James. *Abingdon's Strong's Exhaustive Concordance of the Bible.* Nashville: Abingdon, 1890.

Swindoll, Charles R. *Moses.* Nashville: Word, 1999.

Tada, Joni Eareckson. *When God Weeps.* Grand Rapids: Zondervan, 1997.

Taylor, J. Hudson. *Union and Communion.* London: China Island Mission, 1914.

Tenney, Merrill C., gen. ed. *The Zondervan Pictorial Bible Dictionary.* Grand Rapids: Zondervan, 1967.

Thomas, Gary. *Sacred Marriage.* Grand Rapids: Zondervan, 2000.

Tozer, A. W. *The Knowledge of the Holy.* Lincoln: Back to the Bible, 1961.

Walvoord, John F., and Roy B. Zuck. *The Bible Knowledge Commentary.* Vol. 1. Wheaton, IL: Victor, 1985.

Wiersbe, Warren E., *The Bible Exposition Commentary.* Wheaton, IL: Victor, 1989.

Williams, Margery. *The Velveteen Rabbit.* New York: Barnes & Noble, 1991.

Wolf, Herbert. *Theological Wordbook of the Old Testament.* Chicago: Moody, 1980.

Zacharias, Ravi. *Cries of the Heart.* Nashville: W Publishing Group, 1998.

Zodhiates, Spiros. *The Complete Word Study Dictionary New Testament.* Chattanooga, TN: AMG Publishers, 1992.

Endnotes

Introduction
[1]H.A. Ironside, *Addresses on the Song of Solomon* (New York City: L.B. Printing Co., 1933), 11.

[2]Irving L. Jensen, *Jensen's Survey of the Old Testament* (Chicago: Moody, 1978), 310.

[3]Ibid., 11-12.

Chapter One

[1]Larry Crabb, *Understanding People* (Grand Rapids: Zondervan, 1987), 120.

[2]Philip Carl Weber, *Theological Wordbook of the Old Testament,* vol. 1 (Chicago: Moody Press, 1980), 265.

[3]Tom Gledhill, *The Message of the Song of Songs* (Downers Grove, IL: InterVarsity Press, 1994), 103.

[4]Walvoord and Zuck, 1013.

[5]Walvoord and Zuck, 1014.

[6]John MacArthur, *The Glory of Heaven* (Wheaton: IL: Crossway, 1998), 73.

[7]Unknown Internet source.

[8]Spiros Zodhiates, *The Complete Word Study Dictionary* (Chattanooga: TN: AMG, 1992), 767.

[9]Ephesians 2:4-10, NIV.

[10]Zodhiates, 767.

[11]Ibid., 1265-66.

[12]Ibid., 965.

[13]*The Commercial Appeal*, CAI column, July 26, 2001.

[14]Gleason Archer, R. Laird Harris, and Bruce K. Waltke, *Theological Wordbook of the Old Testament*, vol. 2 (Chicago: Moody, 1980), 701.

[15]Ibid., 433.

[16]Psalm 33:15, NKJV.

[17]I copied this quote in the margin of my Bible. I believe it is from G.K. Chesterton.

[18]Tozer, 41.

[19]Walvoord and Zuck, 1014.

[20]Dan DeHann, *The God You Can Know* (Grand Rapids: Moody, 1982), 139.

[21]Crabb, 37.

[22]F(ranz) Delitzsch, *Proverbs, Ecclesiastes, Song of Solomon,* vol. 6 *Commentary on the Old Testament in Ten Volumes,* by C.F. Keil and F. Delitzsch, trans. by James Martin (Grand Rapids: Eerdmans, 1978 rep.), 46.

[23]Ibid., 46.

[24]Clinton Mack, "Animals of the Bible", in *The Zondervan Pictorial Bible Dictionary*, Merrill C. Tenney, gen. ed. (Grand Rapids: Zondervan, Regency, 1963), 43.

[25]Walvoord and Zuck, 1015.

[26]Philippians 4:6-7, NKJV.

[27]A. W. Tozer, *The Pursuit of God* (Camp Hill, PA: Christian Publications, Inc., 1982, 1993), 22.

[28]Zodhiates, 1246.

[29]*Merriam Webster's Collegiate Dictionary,* 10th ed. (Springfield, MA: Merriam-Webster, 1994), 907.

[30]Zodhiates, 596.

[31]J. Hudson Taylor, *Union and Communion* (London: China Island Mission, 1914), 16.

Chapter Three

[32]Crabb, 44-45.

[33]Ibid., 45.

[34]George Burrowes, *A Commentary on the Song of Solomon* (Edinburgh, Scotland: The Banner of Truth Trust, 1853), 320.

[35]Ibid., 45.

[36]Ibid., 322.

[37]Grant Colfax Tullar, *The Weaver* (Grand Rapids: Faith, Prayer, & Tract League, n.d.).

[38]G. Lloyd Carr, *Song of Solomon* (Downers Grove, IL: Intervarsity Press, 1984), 105.

[39]Burrows, 329-30.

[40]Tom Gledhill, *The Message of the Song of Songs* (Downers Grove, IL: Intervarsity Press 1994), 148.

[41]Ibid.

[42]Charles R. Swindoll, *Moses* (Nashville: Word, 1999), 73.

[43]Matthew 4:1-11, NKJV.

[44]John N. Oswalt, *Theological Wordbook of the Old Testament* (Chicago: Moody, 1980), 149.

[45]Walvoord and Zuck, 1017.

[46]Ibid., 337-8.

[47]George Burrowes, *The Song of Solomon* (London: Billing & Sons Limited, 1853), 336.

[48]R.A. Cole, *The New Bible Dictionary* (Grand Rapids: Eerdmans, 1962), 244.

[49]Othmar Keel, *The Song of Songs* (Minneapolis: Fortress, 1994), 131.

[50]Ibid., 134.

[51]L.M. McPhee, *The Romance of the Ages* (Illinois: Designed Products Inc., 1950), 58.

[52]Exodus 26:31-35; 27:21; 30:6; 35:12; 36:35; 38:27; 39:34; 40:3,21,22,26; Leviticus 4:6,17; 16:2, 12, 15; 21:23; 24:3; Numbers 4:5; 18:7; 2 Chronicles 3:14.

Chapter Four

[53]C.A. Coates, *An Outline of the Song of Songs* (Great Britain: Purnell and Sons, Inc., n.d.), 83.

[54]Burrowes, 349.

[55]Andrew Miller, *Meditations on the Song of Solomon* (London: Walter G. Wheeler, 1877), 139.

[56]Ibid., 140.

[57]Ibid., 140.

[58]Burrowes, 352-3.

[59]Warren E. Wiersbe, *The Bible Exposition Commentary* (Wheaton, IL: Victor, 1989), 603.

[60]Burrowes, 354-5.

[61]Coates, 90.

[62]Loveless, 80.

[63]Zodhiates, 148.

[64]Gledhill, 157.

[65]Burrowes, 358.

[66]Coates, *Outline,* 98.

[67]Ibid.

[68]Gledhill, 157.

[69]Ibid., 158.

[70]Zodhiates, 1306.

[71]Ibid., 1266.

[72]Ibid., 140.

[73]Herbert Wolf, *Theological Wordbook of the Old Testament* (Chicago: Moody Press, 1980), 318.

[74]John N. Oswalt, *Theological Wordbook of the Old Testament* (Chicago: Moody Press, 1980), 100.

[75]Ronald B. Allen, *Theological Wordbook of the Old Testament* (Chicago: Moody Press, 1980), 688.

[76]Leonard J. Coppes, *Theological Wordbook of the Old Testament* (Chicago: Moody Press, 1980), 568-69.

[77]Walvoord and Zuck, 1019.

[78]Loveless, 82.

[79]Ibid., 83.

[80]Ibid., 84.

[81]Ruth Stewart, *Better than Wine* (Asheville, NC: Revival Literature, 1970), 40.

[82]A.W. Tozer, 37.

[83]Gledhill, 165.

[84]Stewart, 42.

[85]Loveless, 86.

Chapter Five

[86]Gledhill, 166.

[87]Othmar Keel, 183-84.

[88]Keel, 188

[89]Revelation 3:20, NKJV.

[90]Gary Thomas, *Sacred Marriage* (Grand Rapids: Zondervan, 2000), 145.

252

[91]Ravi Zacharias, *Cries of the Heart* (Nashville, TN: W Publishing Group, 1998), 132.

[92]Ibid., 137.

[93]Ibid., 140.

[94]McPhee, 70.

[95]Zacharias, 132.

[96]Carr, 137.

[97]John Piper, *A Godward Life* (Sisters, OR: Multnomah, 1997), 34-35.

[98]Ron Dunn, *When Heaven Is Silent* (Nashville, TN: Thomas Nelson, 1994), 124.

[99]Ibid., 124-5.

[100]Ibid.

[101]D.W. Lambert, *Oswald Chambers: An Unbribed Soul* (Pennsylvania: Christian Life Crusade, 1983), 22.

[102]John Piper, *The Hidden Smile of God* (Wheaton: Crossway Books, 2001), 54.

[103]Ibid., 12.

[104]Carmichael.

[105]Joni Eareckson Tada, *When God Weeps* (Grand Rapids: Zondervan, 1997), 84.

[106]Ibid., 12.

[107]Dunn, 38.

[108]Ariel Bloch and Chana Bloch, *The Song of Songs* (New York: Random House, 1996), 184.

[109]Larry Crabb, *Shattered Dreams* (Colorado Springs: Waterbrook Press, 2001), 121.

[110]Ibid., 155-9.

[111]Psalm 84:5-7, NKJV.

[112]Piper, 71.

[113]Ibid., 74-5.

[114]Burrowes, 429.

[115]Ibid., 430.

[116]Ibid.

[117]Ibid., 434.

[118]Ibid., 437.

[119]Bloch and Bloch, 188.

Chapter Six

[120]Philip Yancey, *Where Is God When It Hurts?* (Grand Rapids: Zondervan, 1990), 56.

[121]Joni Eareckson Tada, *When God Weeps* (Grand Rapids: Zondervan, 1997), 155.

[122]G.K. Chesterton.

[123]Piper, *A Godward Life*, 113.

[124]Zacharias, *Cries of the Heart*, 89.

[125]Ibid., 81.

[126]Yancey, 91.

[127]Ibid., 81.

[128]Genesis 41:52, NIV.

[129]Zodhiates, 842.

[130]Ibid., 1313.

[131]Ibid., 1287.

[132]Ibid., 729.

[133]2 Corinthians 1:3-7, NIV.

[134]William J. Peterson, *The Discipling of Timothy* (Wheaton: Victor Books, 1980), 109.

[135]Carr, 145.

[136]Taylor, 56-7.

[137]Burrowes, 448-9.

[138]Carr, 146.

[139]Miller, 238.

[140]Gledhill, 197.

[141]Ibid., 198.

[142]Ibid., 199.

[143]Bloch and Bloch, 194.

[144]Keel, 228.

[145]Miller, 247.

[146]James Strong, *Abingdon's Strong's Exhaustive Concordance of the Bible* (Nashville: Abingdon, 1890).

[147]Keel, 228.

[148]Bloch and Bloch, 194.

[149]Carr, 153.

[150]Bloch and Bloch, 199.

[151]Carr, 153.

[152]Ibid., 154.

Chapter Seven

[153]Bloch and Bloch, 200.

[154]Keel.

[155]Gledhill, 205.

[156]Keel, 231.

[157]Gledhill, 206.

[158]Burrowes, 471.

[159]Ibid., 472.

[160]Keel, 235.

[161]Gledhill, 207.

[162]Bloch and Bloch, 203,

[163]Burrowes, 474.

[164]Ibid., 474.

[165]Zodhiates, 432.

[166]Burrowes, 476.

[167]Keel, 238.

[168]Taylor, 62-3.

[169]McPhee, 91.

[170]Carr, 164.

[171]Keel, 114.

[172]Gledhill, 210.

[173]Bloch and Bloch, 207.

[174]Keel, 252.

[175]Watchman Nee, *Song of Songs* (Fort Washington, PA: Christian Literature Crusade, 1965), 140.

[176]Stewart, 77.

[177]Nee, 142.

[176]Stewart, 77.

[178]Merrill C. Tenney, gen. ed, *The Zondervan Pictorial Bible Dictionary* (Grand Rapids: Zondervan, 1967), s.v., "mandrake."

Chapter Eight

[182]Coates, 199.

[183]J.I. Packer, *Knowing God* (Downers Grove, IL: Intervarsity Press, 1973), 154.

[184]Coates, 65.

[185]Michael D. Goulder, *The Song of Fourteen Songs* (Great Britain: Redwood Burn, Ltd., 1986), 65.

[186]Burrowes, 506.

[187]Ibid., 507.

[188]Bloch and Bloch, 213.

[189]M.M.B., *The Song of Songs* (Pittsburgh, PA: Bethany House, 1944), 188.

[190]Robert Gordis, *The Song of Songs and Lamentations: A Study, Modern Translation, and Comentary*, rev. and augmented ed. (New York: KTAV Publishing House, 1974), 100.

[191]Patterson, 118.

How to order more copies of
Shepherd-Shaped

by Iva May
CALL: 1-800-747-0738
FAX: 1-888-252-3022
Email: orders@hannibalbooks.com
Write: Hannibal Books
P.O. Box 461592
Garland, Texas 75046
Visit: *www.hannibalbooks.com*

Number of copies of *Shepherd-Shaped* _____

Multiply total number of copies: _____ by $12.95 =
Total cost of books: $_____

Add $3 for postage and handling for first book and add
50-cents for each additional book in the order.
Shipping total $_____
Texas residents add 8.25 % sales tax $_____

Total order $_____

number on check enclosed _____
credit card # _____ exp. date_____
(Visa, MasterCard, Discover, American Express accepted)

Name _____

Address _____

City State, Zip _____

Phone _____

Email _____